On the Path of Love
How to Recognize Divine Guidance in Your Life

Jeff and Pam Terrell

Team Terrell Publishing

Team Terrell Publishing
Venice, Florida

Copyright © 2017 Team Terrell
Jeff Terrell and Pam Terrell

This book is a reflection of our own spiritual understandings and is not intended to speak for any spiritual path, teacher, or religion.

All rights reserved. This book may not be reproduced in whole or in part, stored in a retrieval system, or transmitted in any form or by any means electronic, mechanical, or other without written permission from the publisher, except where permitted by law.

Cover design: Pam Terrell

ISBN: 0692890114
ISBN-13: 978-0692890110

This book is dedicated to you.

Sometimes we are aware of it

and other times we are not,

but we are all

On the Path of Love.

CONTENTS

Foreword   vii
Introduction   xi

Part I: The Meeting
1. Girl Meets Boy   15
2. Boy Meets Girl   19

Part II: Pam
3. Growing Up Pam   25
4. Messages to Write   37
5. Life-Changing Inner Message   65
6. Gift of Healing   71

Part III: Jeff
7. Growing Up Jeff   79
8. Lessons From a Past Life   107
9. Knowledge From a Dream   115
10. Power of Thoughts   123

Part IV: A Mission Together
11. A Spiritual Love Story   131
12. Leaving   153
13. The Mission   157

Part V: Epilogue
14. Jeff Shares a Spiritual Exercise   163

Afterward: Coffee Talk with Pam   165

Acknowledgments   167

Jeff & Pam Terrell

FOREWORD

If you've ever wondered if life was a random series of events, then Jeff and Pam's *On the Path of Love* is for you. Have you felt certain events in your life definitely had to happen? Are there people you needed to meet and be with? These moments in eternity can open our awareness of where we came from, and what turns we must make on our own individual path in life to arrive where destiny is guiding us.

Jeff and Pam share their inspiring, wondrous stories and adventures of waking up and recognizing the spiritual connection in all things. Listening to the thoughts, insights, and nudges that miraculously revealed themselves got them to where they had to be; to learn their lessons.

Albert Einstein said, "Example isn't another way to teach, it is the only way to teach." In reading their stories, it becomes clear that we all have the ability to tune-in to this unique guidance to live a more fulfilled life—perhaps even create our own fairy tale.

"Again, you can't connect the dots looking forward; you can only connect them looking backwards. So, you have to trust that the dots will somehow connect in your future. You have to trust in something - your gut, destiny, life, karma, whatever. This approach has never let me down, and it has made all the difference in my life."

—Steve Jobs, Apple co-founder

Jeff and Pam's fairy tale love story is told with the connecting dots revealed. Learning about their path will light up your own creative side—to ask for, and see, the dots that form the stepping stones on your path to serving life.

Looking back and seeing the connecting dots, so to speak, allows them to recognize the divine guidance in their daily lives. Pam and Jeff came to know that destiny is directed by the hand of Divine Spirit.

Travel along on their magical journey spanning hundreds of years to learn about the deeper meaning of life and ultimately Divine Love.

Dr. Jason P. Schwartz
Author, *Fit Into Your Genes, Use Genetics to Achieve Your Healthy Weight*

"According to Greek Mythology, humans were originally created with four arms, four legs and a head with two faces. Fearing their power, Zeus split them into two separate beings, condemning them to spend their lives in search of their other halves."

—*Plato*

INTRODUCTION

"One day I followed a nudge to stand in a particular line. While waiting there, I met someone and instantly the life I knew was forever changed. Our experience together challenged everything I thought was possible, making me believe in the true power of love!"

—Pam Terrell

"When do the events that change your life happen? Where do they occur? It seems so tenuous sometimes—missing a bus by seconds and having to wait for the next one or bumping into someone at the grocery store and noticing how familiar they seem. If I keep my focus on the present moment, I can see the reasons why things happen. Standing in line at the coat check at a spiritual seminar, for instance, is not where one would think a life changing event might occur. You're not at one of the uplifting workshops, roundtables, or discussion groups. You're not at a temple where a magical moment might be expected. Love always happens in the present—so stay there and you never know what you'll find."

—Jeff Terrell

Have you ever felt an unexplained sense of recognition of a person, place, or thing even though it's a new experience? Do you feel your life is being guided instead of a random series of events? Do you feel there is a deeper purpose to your life than you have been able to figure out?

In our book, *On the Path of Love, How to Recognize Divine Guidance in Your Life*, we share our stories of how following our Path of Love helped us to recognize ourselves as Soul, a Divine being. By learning to pay attention to inner guidance, waking and sleeping dreams, intuition, and past life experiences, we were led to physical healing, enlightenment, inner peace, and the knowledge of our life's purpose.

It is our hope that by reading our stories, you will be able to recognize the uplifting miracles within your life as you travel along your own Path of Love.

Jeff & Pam Terrell

Part I:

The Meeting

1

GIRL MEETS BOY

Pam's Experience

Standing in line at the luggage check kiosk wrapped tightly in a soft velvety cape, I sipped black coffee and gazed around the enormous convention center. I saw no warning of the dramatic shift coming within the hour. No flags waved to signal the end of life as I knew it, and no sign stood to welcome a new beginning. Unknowingly, a tornado was ready to rearrange my world and all I had to do was be nice and allow a gentleman to advance in front of me in line.

An hour earlier I was in my hotel room buried in blankets barely able to hear the alarm ring at 7:00 am. It was 33 degrees outside with partly cloudy skies in Minneapolis, Minnesota, which was typical weather for late October. Most of the leaves had fallen from the trees earlier in the month and it felt like winter had arrived. Thankfully, there was no snow in the forecast during my stay.

I was excited about the day ahead but pressed the snooze button on the the alarm to give me five more minutes before it would sound again, just like I did at home. Halfway between the dream and awakened states, I relived the joyful experiences of the weekend. Three days prior I traveled from my home in sunny Florida to attend an annual spiritual seminar with attendees from around the globe. Days were filled with interactive workshops, lively discussion groups, beautiful music, and inspirational guest speakers. I enjoyed conversations with people I knew and also had the pleasure of meeting two new girlfriends. Wonderful memories were made.

Suddenly, I was jolted back to earth as the alarm chimed again. I quickly climbed out of the cozy bed ready to start another magnificent day.

The days had flown by and Sunday morning was upon me. I needed to check-out of the hotel and travel to the convention center for the final few hours of the program. In a blissful daze, I turned on the water to brush my teeth. A peek in the mirror reflected a face I had not seen in a while. Actually, had I ever seen it? Earlier in the month I had completed a healing protocol for an illness I had battled for eighteen years. Eighteen long, dark, and challenging years. I was able to put on my game face around others, but when I looked in a mirror the harsh truth always stared back. However, what I saw *that* morning was pure light and love shining from within. My body was finally healed and I was elated to be alive! I smiled back at the reflection, overcome with immense gratitude.

There was no line at the front desk to check-out so I was ready to catch the shuttle to the convention center. I turned around noticing water pitchers and a very large coffee pot on the counter for hotel guests. I walked over and stood in front of the beverage station contemplating my options. I could have ice water. Or, I could have coffee. Normally I would have water without a second thought. Although I loved the *taste* of coffee, that health crisis had taken it out of my diet plan. However, things were different now. My mind expanded to accept the realization that my body was finally healed and I felt better than I had in two decades. It was cold outside, *I* was cold, I loved the *taste* of coffee, *and* it was right there in front of me. I chose the coffee!

Cup in hand, I lifted the lever and released the warm aromatic brew. I balanced the cup between my hands to warm them while I lifted it to my face—breathing in the exciting smell. I was going to savor that cup of coffee I had waited so many years to indulge in.

I arrived at the convention center focusing on being present to drink in the final experiences around me. As I walked toward the main hall I saw a coat and luggage kiosk to my left. I needed a place to safely stow my suitcase and joined the line.

The escalator on my right traveled up three levels moving visitors to various conference rooms and exhibit halls. Volunteers were bustling to their designated locations and attendees were trickling in. Excitement and peace filled the air. I felt the combination.

What was it? Was it possible to feel peaceful excitement?

Ah, I knew what it was. It was love. I felt the love that permeated the air. And that love swirled around me like a ribbon—protecting me. I was immersed in a supportive safe environment and my heart was open. The ribbon of love sparkled and reflected a beam of light surrounding and guiding me.

I took a drink while patiently waiting. My green eyes peered over the cup and scanned the faces in line. I noticed a gentleman behind me holding a coat. I quickly thought that it would take me longer to check my bag so I should allow him to go in front of me. I turned to the man and said hello. I politely offered for him to go ahead of me since he only had a coat to check and no luggage. He graciously accepted and moved around me. We introduced ourselves and made light conversation. *Jeff*, I repeated his name mentally in an effort to remember it. He stood at the head of the line with his long wool black coat on the counter ready for the next attendant. Leaning against the temporary structure and facing me, he apologized for it taking so long. I heard a voice from the line on my left calling to Jeff. Wow, Judy, one of the two ladies I had met at the seminar was there in line next to us *and* she knew Jeff!

He hung around and talked to me until we completed our transactions. Continuing our discussion would have been enjoyable—but visiting the ladies room before entering the auditorium was *mandatory*. We parted ways and I was left with a puzzled sense of disappointment.

Our conversation wasn't over, yet I watched him walk away.

Moments later, still slightly perplexed about my encounter with Jeff, I breezed through security to enter the auditorium. I moved toward the stage to choose a seat.

In those next few minutes the tornado brewing in the perimeter of my life would set about its mission of rearranging my physical world. Whether realized or not, I was on the path of love. I always had been.

2

BOY MEETS GIRL

Jeff's Experience

Meanwhile, in hotel several blocks away.

𝓙 was sitting at one of the high-top tables in the coffee shop on the first floor of the hotel—fidgeting, I thought they made the chairs uncomfortable intentionally to keep people from staying too long. Regardless, I was enjoying my last few sips of warm creamy coffee before braving the chilly morning air outside. Turning to my left and squinting through the window I saw people outside leaning forward and walking fast. They were wrapped in coats, scarves, and hats attempting to stay warm on their way to their varied destinations. I tapped my cell phone to check the time, thankful I still had a few minutes before I would join them. I savored my last few sips and wiggled in the hard wooden chair. I closed my eyes and took a deep breath. The blank screen of my mind instantly switched on for a moment of silent reflection.

My business trip began nearly a week before when my plane touched down at Lindberg airport in Minneapolis. I rented a car because work took me all the way to Chicago, which was a 7-hour drive. A couple days later I made my way back toward Minneapolis, dodging snowflakes on the highway to arrive in St. Paul. Since my work week ended on Thursday, I decided to take the opportunity to attend a spiritual seminar in Minneapolis. Although the seminar was an annual event, it had been over twenty years since I'd attended one. I was a family man and October was football season. My two sons played from the ages of six all the way through college. They were quite talented and it was a joy to watch them. The years passed quickly and in the blink of an eye my boys were all grown up and football in the fall was in my rear-view mirror. I'm thankful I could share those special years with my family. I was sad it was over but then realized I was free to attend the seminar.

I heard conversation from a couple at my table and was brought back into the present moment. I stared at my empty coffee cup, silently wishing for just one more sip of the marvelous liquid. I checked the time again then gathered my things. It was the third and final day of the big event and I did not want to be late. I stuffed my laptop into the black leather briefcase and slid my cell phone into my right front jean pocket.

Even though I had a car, I had been making the five-block trip back and forth to the convention center daily on foot. The silver Spark rental car was safely tucked away in the parking garage by the hotel. I stood near the exit door and fastened the top button of my coat. It took a moment to brace myself for the chilly wind I knew would greet me outside.

Although I have always lived in cold climates like Pennsylvania and Virginia, the brisk wind hit hard that morning against my unprotected face. Along the front of the hotel a row of decorative flags flew high above the street. The sound of the fabric flapping against the poles was deafening in the high wind. That sound served to indicate a strong headwind but it also lifted my spirits. It served as a reminder that I was on my way to a wonderful spiritual adventure.

I am not usually a fast walker but arrived at the front doors to the convention center in record time. I made my way in and stepped aside, appreciating the warm still air.

Suddenly, too suddenly, it was Sunday morning and I faced the last few hours of the phenomenal seminar. I had waited a very long time to get to that point and as I mulled it over, it seemed like an eternity. I looked back upon my life. The previous twenty-plus years were a blur, yet at the same time it seemed like it had been a very long time since I stood in the Minneapolis Convention Center at a seminar. The juxtaposition of those two perspectives jolted my awareness and I shuddered. Not due to the cold, but rather the stark realization of what that moment offered. I stood, transfixed, drinking in the moment in all its glory. I was there, finally!

The moment caught up with me as I took a step forward, returning to the flow of life on the physical plane. I was excited about the days' events but also trepidatious it would soon be over and time to return home. I began thinking about my schedule. After the seminar, I had a thirty-minute drive to the airport. Once there I could relax an hour or so before the flight to Pennsylvania took off. I would also have some downtime on the plane. That buffer between the soulful experiences of the seminar and the harsh realities of daily life was a blessing.

I walked at a much slower pace since I was inside enjoying the warmth. I noticed the vastness of the convention center and the hundreds of attendees mulling around as they began their day. I became present with my surroundings and stopped thinking about the end of the seminar. After all, there were still a few hours with speakers, music, stories, and friends left to experience.

I pondered whether to check my coat or haul it into the auditorium. The morning program was only a few hours so it did not make sense to bother waiting in a long line. But since I wasn't in a hurry *and* I was enjoying the morning experiences, I figured I would go ahead and check it. I was walking along the corridor toward the main hall when I made my decision. Instantly, I looked to my left and saw a coat check station with only a few people waiting. Perfect. It was a good thing I was paying attention or I might have missed it.

I hung a quick left and joined the line.

I heard a woman's voice in front of me say, "Hello, you only have a coat and I have a bag so please go ahead of me."

"Oh, thank you, I really appreciate it", I said.

I stepped in front of the woman and hefted my coat from my shoulders and placed it on the counter. The ladies at the coat check were busy so I took that opportunity to look around. I caught eyes with the woman who offered me her place in line. I thanked her again for allowing me in front of her and then apologized for it taking so long. She assured me she was in no hurry.

Little did I know, but that interaction was the beginning of a major life-change. In the following hour, I would have an experience that would alter the course of my future. Everything in my current life would be thrust upon the bonfire of change—my twenty plus year marriage, my job, where I lived, and how I felt about myself and my life.

The wind of change was blowing through me as strongly as the wind had blown the flags outside of my hotel that morning.

Part II: Pam

Jeff & Pam Terrell

3

Growing Up Pam

My First Inner Guidance Message

*L*essons appear on our path to help teach about life, love, and ourselves. It took many years, and an unforgettable event, to understand the value of listening—on the outer *and* the inner.

I was an extremely shy child known to hide behind my mothers' legs when strangers approached. I was most comfortable playing alone, perhaps because no girls my age lived nearby. A few years of elementary school cured the shyness, though, evolving me into a happy content child.

I lived in Missouri in an average middle-class neighborhood with my dad, mom, and older brother. My family seldom attended church nor talked about God at home. There were no prayers before dinner or bedtime and no Bible readings. In fact, my earliest church memory was participating in vacation Bible school with my best friend. We attended different elementary schools but over summer break her mom babysat me and my brother and I got to see her every weekday. The church program lasted one week and included artsy activities. The creative projects were fun but the teachings were confusing. I memorized verses from the Bible for homework assignments but the words and meaning were not clear. I enjoyed the session, however, because I was with my dear friend.

My parents divorced when I was fourteen and I lived with my mother. Strangely, I was not sad about their separation. In fact, when they broke the news I was relieved. Quite relieved. I may have been young, but they were not happy together and somehow I knew things were not the way they should be in a marriage.

I was independent and felt a separation between children and parents; I did my thing and they did theirs. Our interaction was mainly during meal times and besides going to work, I had no idea how they spent their time. I did not confide in them about my personal dilemmas. I mean, I was a kid—they were adults. And if I needed help, I certainly did not know how to ask for it. I never learned that. I did, however, learn to figure things out myself. Oh, and how to be alone.

Teenage years were a perplexing mix of excitement muddled with confusion. I hold fond memories of cheerleading, singing in choir concerts, and close friendships that shaped me into a confident individual. I learned about boys and the emotions accompanying those relationships. By the time the sun shined on my sixteenth year the innocent happy days were over. In stark contrast, high school seemed full of disappointment as I experienced the highs and lows in life for the first time. I was no longer sheltered by my parents from the real world's painful lessons. Although these were typical adolescent dramas, I was emotionally sensitive and impacted on a deep level. Cheating and lies ran rampant—my heart did not understand such things. I was left shaken with doubt of people's motives and showed minimal trust in their words.

It was during those years when I first experimented with alcohol and cigarettes. I was home alone for a couple hours before my mom returned from work so snuck out a few ounces of liquor from the meager bar. I was smart, though, and refilled the Vodka or Gin with an equal amount of water in case they knew how much was in each bottle. I quickly drank it down straight to get the most effect, then put on headphones cranked up with Boston, Steely Dan, or Peter Frampton records. I got in a quick nap before mom arrived to sleep off any effects of the drink, so I could keep my secret. At some point, I increased the amount I drank because, remember, some of the bottle contained water from me refilling it so much. Of course, kids snuck alcohol into parties and I would partake. Periodically I would cross a thin line and have a few sips before school when I caught a ride with friends who had a bottle of something. Anything.

Drinking alcohol was not a learned behavior, I never saw it at home. But somehow, I felt the escapism it provided from the first time it passed my lips. High school graduation day could not come fast enough. I was not sad or depressed, just simply trying to maneuver life.

I did not search for a religious or spiritual path, nor have an inquisitive nature about religion or God. I attended church periodically with a couple of high school girlfriends, so was aware there were many teachings. I always enjoyed the various services but never felt I was a member, nor had interest in being one.

When I was seventeen my life took a crucial turn after a realization shifted my awareness—and my future. What started out as typical spring day turned into something far from it.

I was up and about early Saturday morning. Meandering toward my car, I pulled my arms through a sweater, thankful to no longer need a bulky coat. The chill in the air was refreshing. Winter was on its way out and sunny warm days lay ahead. The grass below my feet was no longer hard, lifeless, and brown but instead soft and coming alive. Dew covered the blades as specks of green shimmered in the sunlight. Lifting my head slightly, I admired the azure sky scattered with feathery white clouds lit up by a brilliant sun. Yes, spring had sprung. I slowly inhaled, filling my lungs with the vibrant energy.

I climbed into my car and let the engine warm up before taking off toward the highway entrance a short mile away. I switched off the radio dial seeking peace and quiet. It was time to figure something out. My concentration on driving was distracted as tears of frustration welled up inside. My mind was reeling. I had a problem—a *big* problem. I pondered a situation in which my mother wanted me to do one thing, my father another, and my instincts were guiding me toward a totally different answer. The pit in my stomach trembled in confusion.

How was I to make everyone happy?

The question hung over my head in a huge stormy gray cloud. I continued pondering each scenario for several minutes, but no matter how I tried, there seemed to be no way of making everyone happy.

Suddenly, the cloud over my head exploded! I was jolted upright. My body was alert and stiff like a soldier standing at attention while seated behind the steering wheel.

Swirling and surrounding me in a strong, loving, and forceful voice, I heard:

"You can't please everyone, you are going to have to please yourself".

The sentence consumed my head and pushed out all other thoughts.

You can't please everyone, you are going to have to please yourself, was telling me to trust my instincts, my intuition. That strong feeling inside I could not shake no matter how much my mind tried.

In that moment, I experienced my first feeling of "knowingness". My life was being guided and I needed to pay attention. The words I heard are music lyrics from the 1970's "Garden Party" song by Ricky Nelson, but there was no song being sung. The radio was off.

It was the powerful and exacting way the words landed in my consciousness that I knew, 1) they were truth, and 2) they were meant for me. Yes, the words were meant for *me*.

It was as if I'd remembered something I already knew. Somehow, I was aware of something to be truth although I did not read or study about it, instead the feeling and sense of truth needed no proof.

I did not doubt the answer I got and, in fact, no longer thought about the predicament I was vacillating over. On that magical morning, I heard my first divine guidance message loud and clear!

From that day on I lived my life more intuitively. I stopped over-thinking and learned to trust feelings for guidance. Daily experiences became more relevant. Each emotional high or low was a stepping stone and as long as I chose to see the lesson, instead of viewing myself as a victim, there was no need to manifest the same thing twice. If I learned—then I got to move on to something else.

I was only seventeen years old when awakened by the words that exploded in my mind and landed softly in my heart. It was quite a blessing for a teenager to have such a valuable tool at their disposal. Divine guidance would speak to me many more times, so thankfully I learned to recognize it. And listen to it.

A Gift Resolves Fear

I began trusting my instincts after receiving the divine guidance message in my car. Four years later a strong familiar feeling persuaded me to go out on an ordinary night—which led to an extraordinary chain of events.

My friend and I arrived at the dance club after midnight Friday night. The parking lot was packed so I was relieved we rode together and only had to find one parking space. I had not put much effort into anything that night. I had oscillated whether to go out and when the decision was finally made there was only time to throw on casual clothes, run a brush through my hair, and freshen eye makeup. Normally I would have given my appearance more time and attention, but for some reason I did not want to go out—but felt I *should*. I was nudged and it was strong enough I had to pay attention.

Once inside the loud bustling room we made a bee-line to an open table. Although only of legal drinking age for a few months, I had gotten to know lots of people who loved dancing and live music as much as me. I surveyed the room and spotted a couple familiar faces. I made my way over to say hello and they introduced me to a man sitting with them. His name was Dean and we immediately struck up conversation. I sat in an extra chair at their table and hung out for a few hours until the bartender announced closing time. That was disappointing; I was having a great time. My friends and I were not ready to call it a night so the party moved to someone's house. The friend I had ridden with had joined us for a while but left an hour earlier, leaving me with no car. I needed a ride to the party so opted to tag along with Dean.

We stayed about two hours until it got to be very early in the morning and clearly time to head home. He gave me a lift to where I had parked my car hours earlier and before parting ways asked me out on a proper date. I accepted.

The next day I felt jittery, knowing our connection was different than any I had experienced. I sensed an indescribable recognition; we were supposed to meet and somehow, I knew that was the reason I needed to go out.

Our date on Sunday went well and another was planned. When the doorbell rang the following night, I greeted him with a quick hug then noticed he had something in his hand. He reached out offering me a book. He told me if I was going to date him then I should know about his beliefs. I gracefully accepted and placed it on the coffee table for later reading. Leaving the gift behind, we headed to dinner.

The following work day was busy, which helped time pass quickly. I was anxious to read the book after the statement he made when he gave it to me. "I needed to know about his beliefs"—that sounded kind of dramatic, didn't it?

Once home I filled a kettle with water and placed it on the stove. A little herbal tea would nicely set the mood. As the water heated I headed into the bedroom to get out of my dress and heals and into comfy sweatpants and a t-shirt. Seated on the edge of the bed, I reached down for my fuzzy slippers. I was startled by a roaring whistle and hurried into the kitchen to turn off the burner, silencing the kettle. I chose a mint tea bag, placed it in my favorite mug, and poured in the boiling water to steep. I grasped the mug between my hands allowing the steam to fill my senses and headed into the living room.

I was donning the proper attire to snuggle in with a blanket and a good book. Feelings of fatigue alternated with fluttering butterflies in my core. It had been an eventful week and I was happy to finally relax and see what the mysterious book in my hands was about.

The cover mentioned a spiritual journey. I was curious and revealed the first pages. Immediately intriguing was her writing style. The author wrote directly to the reader, like a letter to a friend, as if she was having a private conversation. Her personal touch quickly lured me in. I consumed page after page in awe of the amazing information and how her words spoke directly to me.

How could she know how I felt and what questions were in my mind?

How did she write this letter of love to me?

I had acquired an amazing gift. I was blown away how one little book could answer every spiritually related question I had *ever* thought about—why we are here on this earth, how to recognize guidance, and what happens when we die.

A wave of shock vibrated through me from head to toe as I read about reincarnation, the rebirth of Soul in a new body. I had struggled with an intense fear of death since I was a child. My eyes drifted off the page as a flashback transported me to a haunting scene from my youth.

I hid on the floor in the closet soaked in tears and paralyzed with fear. Breathing was laborious but I needed to stay quiet enough to not be heard; I knew that much. No one was to know about the struggle and turmoil my mind endured. No one.

I knew where the fear came from. A cold suppressed memory found me on a church pew a year prior. The thunderous man on stage ranted about Heaven and Hell; mostly Hell. His fiery words were not nearly as strong as the emotional energy within them. Intense overwhelming terror filled every cell in my childish body as I listened to the sermon. If what I heard was true, then when I died I would go to either Heaven or Hell, depending on if I did what that man instructed, along with attend church—*their* church. Even scarier was the thought I would never be alive again. Ever. I could not figure that out.

How could I be alive one minute and then gone forever?

Forever was such a long time. The world had gone on for years and would continue for many more, yet I would never, ever be alive again. Unfathomable.

I was just an eight-year-old kid and such information seemed quite a heavy burden to accept. In the backseat during the drive home from church I surmised that if I never died, I would never go to Heaven, or risk going to Hell. A legitimate plan, I thought.

The forceful words were burned into my brain and during the following year the thought of dying sometimes immobilized me. As I innocently played with my dolls and reenacted a scene from a movie where a man died, a full-fledged panic attack ensued. The thought of death entered my mind and prompted a chemical reaction that fired up the memory of the Heaven and Hell sermon. The passion, energy, and panic ignited as my mind got high jacked—consumed with the words, *I will never be alive again, ever.*

I will never be alive again, EVER.

Each repetition fueled the flame of fear. Holding back explosive tears, I crawled into the basement coat closet in my playroom. I knew the only way to fight the attack was to hide away and battle my mind's evil thoughts.

Intense stress welled up as I fought the horrendous images and words from the sermon. I envisioned years and years passing by without me. I would be dead and gone, never to be on the planet again.

What was the point of life if I was only going to be around for such a short time? Why was I even here?

Consumed in darkness, the words repeated gaining strength and momentum.

I will never be alive again, ever, played continuously. They spiraled around my head expanding into an unending deep vortex; a tunnel. The negative force was sucking the child out of me. I had to get control—control of my mind. I was aware enough to know I had to STOP the thoughts. Although I had done it several times since hearing the sermon, they were stronger that day.

I had to STOP THE SENTENCE from repeating.

I am here now, I told myself.

I am HERE, now.

I am HERE NOW.

I AM HERE NOW.

I-AM-HERE-NOW, I screamed to myself!

Slowly those words captured my consciousness and began dissipating the formidable negative force trying to take hold of me. Sitting on the green shag carpet hidden under coats hanging above, light began to shine on my closed eyelids. Threads of golden light gently peeped through in brilliant rays breaking up the darkness blocking them. I repeated the comforting line for a few long moments until gold light had erased all the darkness.

Not wanting to be discovered, I crawled from the closet fatigued and lifeless. I lay on the floor beside my doll village, exhausted. I had won the battle. I had focused on the present moment, the now. All visions and fears of the unknown were destroyed and there was only the moment at hand.

Warm white loving light enveloped me. I knew I was safe.

Mint tea filled my senses. I shuddered and drew a long deep breath. Slowly my eyes opened and regained focus. The book had fallen from my lap onto the floor and I reached down to retrieve it. I returned to the page and reread her words about reincarnation. My mind expanded and began firing on all cylinders. As the pages turned I *knew* it was my truth. I wasn't learning something new, instead I was remembering what I *already* knew.

Elation erupted inside as I read chapter two about her personal description of how she first experienced "knowingness". She spoke of waking up one morning and suddenly understanding reincarnation. One day she didn't know it and the following day she did. It was that simple. Her words were profound.

Time stalled.

I continued reading about life, death, and reincarnation. The words revealed a profound knowingness of my own. Suddenly, I understood. I *knew* about reincarnation. There was no reason to be afraid of death! Emotions bubbled to the surface and released in streams along my cheeks. With a snap of a finger I was no longer afraid of dying. The fear I had endured for thirteen years was replaced with a peaceful loving presence in my heart. In awe, I also knew my life had purpose. I did not think I was actively searching for God or a spiritual path, but thankfully it found me.

I was twenty-one when I read my first spiritual book and remembered what I already knew. The cascade of events that led to my awakening was nothing short of miraculous; the knowledge of staying in the present moment to conquer fear while hiding in the closet, a divine guidance message in my car, the strong nudge to go out, the gift from Dean, and the conquered fear of death. I was on a road filled with lessons and experiences I needed to open my heart to God's love.

4

MESSAGES TO WRITE

It Begins with Journaling

I continued studying spiritual books but reading alone was not going to get me where I needed to go. I was learning about personal physical signs that can appear during our daily lives to help guide our way, referred to as waking dreams. Then there was golden-tongued wisdom, a way of guidance through words that are spoken, either directly to us or something said around us, usually while we are pondering a question. I was about to experience these signs first-hand, quickly realizing if I ignored one message, then another perhaps stronger and louder one, would find me.

Dean and I married a year after we met and by 1992, I was twenty-seven with an energetic five-year-old son, Alex. Awakening on the inner left me unbalanced in the outer world—discontent living on this planet and contemplating the direction I should head spiritually.

What was I doing? Was I living my passion?

When I was young I fantasized about what I would do when I grew up. *Would I be a poet? A singer? A musician?* I wrote poetry in my teens seeing how it helped flesh out emotions. Someday, I had hoped to combine my love of words and music into songs.

I was not a song writer, though. Instead, I worked an office job 9-5, enjoyed classes at the gym after work, and spent time with family.

Why wasn't I content?

I had not been myself at work during the past week and co-workers noticed. The usual happy and pleasant voice that answered the telephone was distant and lifeless. I was grumpy, easily agitated, and clueless why I was feeling that way. Not wanting to spend another work day in agony, I called Dean to get some advice. Instead of giving me his opinion of what was wrong, he shared a simple technique he had used in the past which might help me get my own personal answer. Insight from within.

He recommended I write down exactly how I felt. I did not understand nor comprehend what he meant.

"You mean like write a story?", I asked.

He told me to just start writing about how I felt and if I had any thoughts about the reason why—assuring me the words would begin to flow. He seemed quite confident, yet did not push too hard. I was intrigued and decided to give it a whirl. What did I have to lose?

After grabbing pen and paper I stepped away from my desk and found a quiet spot at a small table in the break room, facing a wall to avoid any eye contact. I stared blankly at the empty page before me. After a few moments, I placed my pen on the paper and magic began to happen. Believe it or not, he was right! Thoughts raced into my mind as I attempted to capture them onto the page. I wrote quickly with no filter or interpretation. Frustration and confusion were laid out on the white sheet before me until my mind was clear—all the words had been written. I breathed a sigh of relief noticing a lightness within. I looked at my watch and noticed only five minutes had passed. But what had I written? I started at the beginning and read what my hand had unconsciously penned, surprised to find that inside the first paragraph was the reason for my uncharacteristic mood. My own words spoke to me with the answer needed.

The balance I was seeking with spirituality while living

on this planet would become clearer as I gained life experience. If I attended spiritual services weekly it would strengthen my connection to God, or the Holy Spirit, and help guide me forward. Once I knew the answer, it was strange to need such a dramatic experience for what seemed to be an obvious solution.

Writing enabled me to step outside of the situation and view it from another perspective. It also emptied all thoughts and confusion out of my head—creating space—space for answers to fall into.

It seemed too good to be true; all I had to do was write and answers would fall onto the page before me. What an amazing tool I had been given.

A couple days later I experienced another emotional meltdown. During a similar discussion with Dean, I admitted still feeling bored and unfulfilled. Life seemed so menial. I admitted, I had not attended any events since getting the message during the first writing exercise. Once again, he suggested I write about what I was feeling. I did not have time at that exact moment because I was preparing to leave for a weekly HU Song. I made a mental note to write later when I got home.

There was nothing like a HU Song to lift my spirits. I was thankful to join several others to share in the love song to God.

The sound is HU, pronounced like the man's name Hugh, spoken or sung in a long drawn out breath. It's an ancient universal name for God, known since early man. Singing HU for twenty minutes daily can deepen your understanding of what is going on in your life by opening your awareness to a higher viewpoint. If times are hard, HU can align you with the Holy Spirit. It is a non-directed prayer inviting God's will to be done, instead of thy own will.

I considered skipping the meeting after my emotionally exhausting day; that is until Connie, who led the event, called to inform me she had a book order for my husband.

Dean handled purchasing of materials so it looked like I needed to go and get the order for him. I was being pushed out the door no matter how tired I felt.

Backing my car out of the garage, I noticed rain drizzle landing on the windshield. Knowing the water would not freeze was a comfort. Alex was in back on the passenger side strapped into the booster seat where I could easily see him. He often attended events. I liked the idea of having him with me in the uplifting environment, only needing to pack coloring books and a few of his favorite toys to keep him occupied. If the roads were a danger, we would have stayed home.

We sang aloud to some of our favorite songs on the radio for the short twenty-minute drive. We arrived a few minutes before the meeting began and I heard people discussing a story Connie was writing for a newsletter. I hurried to situate Alex in the adjacent room then returned to locate a seat. The meeting began and the focus was on the HU.

I closed my eyes gently placing my attention into the third eye, located between the eyebrows above the nose. I sang in a long drawn out breath along with several others in the room. The sound was beautiful, relaxing, and exactly what was needed to shed the weight from my workday. My objective wasn't to push all thoughts away, but instead create space in my mind in case there were answers waiting for me. I heard the closing words, and reluctantly brought myself back onto the planet. *Had it been twenty minutes already?*

Afterwards, discussion resumed regarding the future story for the newsletter. I paid attention, very interested in learning what she was working on. Connie looked across the room—directly at me—and said, "*You* would be a good one to write on that subject matter!"

Startled, looking to my left then right to verify she was, in fact, talking to me. The comment was so unexpected. It made me feel good, even though she had no idea if I could write. *Or, did she?*

The meeting was wrapping up and I noticed Connie had a hard cover book under her overstuffed leather purse sitting on the floor. She pulled it out to return to an attendee. Not wanting to be nosey, I glimpsed at the book in her hands then quickly looked away. I did not catch the exact title but I clearly saw the word: WRITING.

What was going on? It seemed the world was speaking to me—trying to get my attention.

Although I was perplexed by the meaning of the evening events, Alex and I gathered his things and said our farewells to our friends. Snug inside the car for the ride home, I pondered what I had witnessed while Alex dozed off.

Once on the highway, I was alert. The only car I ever noticed on the roads were Buicks. At night when the lights were on, the red tail lights stretched all the way across the back and looked classy, which is part of the reason I owned one. I don't think I would have noticed any other car, let alone a license plate.

Traveling in the center lane on a dimly lit highway road, I looked into the passenger mirror and saw a silver car moving quickly. They were driving extremely fast and passed me. I knew they should not have passed on my right so I looked their direction, as if to scold them. They had already breezed by and all I could see was the back of the car—it was a Buick. Cool lights, indeed!

I looked down below the bright red blur of tail lights noticing their license plate spelled out a word, instead of the typical jumbled letters and numbers. I always enjoyed deciphering vanity plates. However, as the car hovered in front of mine, I saw a word that needed no decoding.

It read: WRITING.

I kid you not! Laughter spilled out loud it was so funny. I felt quite silly to need an answer written out so bluntly for me to get the message.

The remaining drive home seemed to take only minutes. Once inside, I tucked my son lovingly into his bed because I had something very important to do.

After quietly making my way downstairs to my computer desk, I sat down and wrote about the events of the night. I was using my new tool I hoped would help answer my questions within—WRITING.

The multiple messages I attained that one single night were crystal clear and quite astounding. The golden-tongued wisdom of Dean saying to write and Connie recommending I write, along with the waking dreams of Connie's book order, Connie's book about writing, and the license plate that said WRITING, were clear messages showing me my path.

The longer I study spiritual topics, the more aware I become of how divine spirit works in my life. Sometimes I am able to recognize and follow the guidance immediately, yet other times I may need multiple signs to help me learn to trust the messages presenting themselves. Perhaps you have seen words on a billboard along the road which happened to answer a question you had been perplexed by. Or maybe you have read a random sentence from a book while contemplating a situation in your mind; inside the sentence was a clue for your next step. The signs are all around us, just waiting to be discovered.

My eighteen-year health struggle had not yet begun. First, I needed to learn about the power of writing. I was going to need this effective tool to help gain spiritual insight, trust the road being laid out before me, and journal my experiences along the way. Only then could my true purpose and mission become clear.

First Messages to Write a Book

My thirtieth year was pivotal, leading me onto a harrowing path containing some tough lessons; what I had agreed to learn before this lifetime began. Sometimes the most painful circumstances teach us the most. I'm thankful I did not realize ahead of time what I had in store because I would have wanted to call it quits. I did not anticipate the dark days, turning into years, of emotionally and physically draining health struggles to be endured. However, a strong force pushed me forward, even when I had nothing left to give. I would live to tell the painful story thanks to a powerful inner drive and belief that discourages suicide because if I ended my life, I would have to come back and do it all over again. Now that would defeat the purpose, wouldn't it?

Morning was arduous; I had to leave the dream state behind. I liked sleeping—a lot. Dreaming, not feeling a physical body. Flying, spreading my arms, knowing I could travel above the trees. To view the crooked branches covered with green leaves as I rose above them, higher and higher. Into the sky, I flew like a jet plane. I could imagine a place and appear in the scene without a care of where I was going, just up and away. There was an enjoyable sense of limitlessness which contradicted the immense weight when I would return to my human body. It was quite magical and I wanted to stay, forever. *Please don't bring me back to the physical world.*

The alarm gently welcomed me back as I reluctantly pried my sleepy eyes open. I admired the beautiful scene on the bedroom wall—sideways, actually. It was a wallpaper mural Dean put up allowing me to see an uplifting picture when I woke up. One entire wall was filled with a view from nature. The picture was taken above a large lake where many multi-colored red, yellow, and green hot air balloons drifted high into the cloudless blue sky. Tears touched the pillow as I began to feel the body surrounding me. Yes, the headache I had endured for seven years was still throbbing. Swallowing, trying to contain the tears, I felt the burning in back of my throat. It had been five years with a throat on fire: constantly, non-stop. Every moment of every day my head pounded and my throat screamed. Today was to be no different. Feelings emerged in the rest of my body; from head to toe I ached. The blood and lymph under my skin pulsed toxic sludge through my veins. I felt it; the heat, the swelling. The inability of my body to shed the toxins and heal.

I sobbed uncontrollably. *Really? Still?* I was exhausted at the thought of surviving another day. I had just woken up after twelve hours of sleep, which is when healing is supposed to happen, and felt just as badly as when I had crawled into bed. Each night I hoped that after enough rest I would wake up feeling better. But no matter how much I slept, I woke up each morning feeling terrible. Morning and sunrise, to me, meant having to start all over again with another challenging day to get through.

I cried awhile; for strength. My physical body contained no energy and I had learned to rely on my mind to take up the slack. Positive words filled my brain.

I can do this. I'm going to be okay. I have energy, I told myself.

Squeezing fortitude from deep within my core to fuel the thoughts, my mind and body finally aligned enough for me to crawl out of bed. It would take an hour some days to psych myself up enough to get my body moving. A truly daunting and depressing feeling; which was why I dreaded mornings.

I had two hours to get ready for work. Luckily my starting time was later so I could have a little more sleep and less stress. I was blessed that on some of the days I worked, my husband and son got themselves ready and off to work and school without me. As I made my way into the kitchen, I heard music coming from the living room. I paused to listen. James Taylor. Yes, JT sang "Secret of Life", with a voice that touched my heart. Dean had set the stereo to play and repeat one of my favorite songs when he left for work. That way, when I finally made it out of the bedroom I would hear music to cheer me up. I was touched, feeling the love in his efforts.

I knew he felt helpless. And I certainly was not able to be the wife and mother I wanted to be, and knew I could be. I kept so much darkness inside. I did not want to be sick and the person who talked about how bad they felt, nor the one who looked pathetic and helpless. No, if I was going to be sick, then I would stay busy putting on an award-winning facade. No one would know the sad, lonely, painful truth.

I had exhausted all traditional medical resources within a few years and stumbled upon an advertisement for a holistic doctor. No physician had heard me and I was desperate. I always posed questions on the inner, during my HU or contemplation, asking for answers. I agreed I would do whatever I needed to do to heal; just please let me know what was wrong. And what I needed to do. I would do it. Period.

I decided to give the alternative doctor a try. During my initial consultation, I sat across from him and expressed how I felt. On the inside. On the outside.

Within five minutes he said, "Your liver doesn't seem to be working well enough."

What?

I was frozen. Speechless.

After five years of tests, prodding, and no concrete answers to my medical condition, I was finally given actual information. I *knew* his words were true. They may not have been proven by science, but I knew.

Detox began and even though I didn't think I could feel any worse, I did. The protocol was correct, I just knew it. However, I was the only one who felt that way and eventually I decided to shut myself off from the outside world. Family and friends thought I was crazy to continue an alternative route and were genuinely concerned. It did not help when I could not conceal the discomfort one day while at a sporting event of my son's. Led to the car for a reprieve by Dean and my best friend, I cried and writhed in pain in the backseat. An hour later sweet sleep gave me temporary escape. They begged me to stop the nutrition supplements—but I felt I had no choice but to proceed forward.

I cried, every day, at least once. Therapeutic, perhaps, a coping mechanism to release stress.

I worked with the holistic doctor to heal my body and eventually left the stressful full-time job I was trying to uphold and joined his office staff on a part-time basis. He guided me toward healing, phase one.

Months passed showing steady progress. Eventually I categorized myself as 70% well and could function in the outside world I had detached from. The learning curve to health was a steep one. I had not lived a healthy lifestyle, especially in my twenties, nor realized its importance. A decade of smoking cigarettes, drinking plenty of alcohol, and having no regard of my food choices led to my bodies' demise. The alternative doctor assured me I did not cause it, he said everyone has a weak organ and mine was the liver. Although I had stopped drinking and smoking when I turned thirty, damage done did not heal overnight.

The realization I may have caused the damage myself was staggering. But I owned it. I let myself know that I may have caused the ailments when I did not know better, and it was okay—if I learned from it. I took ownership of the current situation and internally asked for help to rectify my health, and my life. I was 70% well—but that wasn't good enough. That was not it. I could be better. Feel better. I *knew* I was going to get better. So, I pushed forward.

An actual roller coaster ride would have been more fun than having your life imitate one. In the beginning of the illness almost all days were bad ones, perhaps a good day was sprinkled in for good measure. During detox, days were also bad but good ones appeared more frequently, and came in pairs. When I reached the 70% mark, good days outnumbered the bad, which was a vast improvement. Life was still dipping, climbing, peaking, and falling, but in stages I was more able to emotionally handle.

I tried everything that crossed my path and made sense.

Food and nutrition seemed paramount so I began by removing preservatives and food additives, moving toward a clean whole food diet; then switched to vegetarian; segued to veganism; which led directly into the raw food world.

One day Dean came home from work early and told me he had some bad news. Emotional, he said his job was being transferred so he either needed to find a new one or move to Florida. I listened as he spoke but could not figure it out.

"What's the bad news?", I asked.

A few short months later I left Kansas, along with my old home, life, and doctor who set me upon my health journey. We were Florida bound!

The plane landed at the Tampa airport on a January morning. As we exited onto the jetway the first breathe of warm, humid, salty southern air filled my lungs. Instantly, I felt I was born and raised in the wrong state. I was finally home; my home was in Florida!

Life in Florida

Raw food and Florida went hand in hand. I embraced the lifestyle witnessing positive shifts in my health and well-being. Alex entered high school and Dean enjoyed his new office. After settling in for a few years I found spiritually open-minded friends interested in healthy living also. Toni and I worked together a couple years but only saw each other in the office. We had an opportunity to chat one afternoon and realized many common interests. Our time together expanded to include some social events focusing on being present and living in the moment.

During dinner together one evening, we delved into personal stories. Toni spoke of her late-mother, Catherine. Although no longer physically walking the earth, Toni explained how she had been leaving dimes for her through the years. They were left in various, yet meaningful, places as a way of letting Toni know everything was going to be okay on that path; whatever the situation. Her mom was communicating with her even after her death. I was moved by her intimate story.

The next morning, I got up as usual, readied for work, and headed out the door toward my car parked along the street. I reached out to unlock the door when something on the ground caught my eye. It was not shiny and clean. It did not glisten in the sun. No sparkles made it stand out from the filthy road it sat on. It was not even easy to see, but for some reason I looked down and there it was—a dime! It was directly in my path on the street.

Immediately Toni's story popped into my mind. I had just heard it the night before, and first thing in the morning light *I* found a dime. There was no other change around it, just the single coin. In awe, I reached down to retrieve it and feel the metal between my fingers to confirm it was real.

At that moment, I became a true believer. I mean, I *believed* the story the night before, but the personal experience helped me understand it first-hand. To share my excitement, I dialed Toni on my cell. The phone rang, one—two—three rings. I second guessed the timing of my call and hoped I was not disturbing her morning routine. A "hello" came though the line—but she already knew. She saw my name on her caller ID and predicted what I was going to say. How did she know? Because the rest of the story is that everyone she tells it to—that believes—starts finding dimes along *their* path!

The story was a gift to help on my journey. Dimes appearing became my waking dream symbol that physically showed up and relayed a message of confirmation. They tell me, "you're on the right path" and I am at peace knowing all is as it should be. No need to worry about a correct decision or rethink a choice already made, it is crystal clear to move on in peace. Knowing you are on the right path in life can be most valuable.

My spiritual path was progressing along quite well and I was making changes in my personal life to reduce stress and figure out how to heal my ailing body the rest of the way. I was on a serious mission to heal. Although dreading it, I knew it was time to have a difficult discussion with Dean. We tried to do most things together as a couple but I was learning about alternative health options I was drawn to investigate, which were things he had no interest in. There were lectures and food demonstrations I wanted to attend but I needed to feel comfortable going alone. I called him to discuss my feelings. I asked for his support and for the freedom to do some things separately in the future. He understood and was agreeable because he wanted me to be healthy.

When I got off the phone I felt better. I had made a decision to improve my health, implemented it, and had a difficult discussion behind me. Quite relieved, I walked into the garage to finish doing laundry. As I walked across the cool gray cement floor toward the washer, I saw something shiny to my left in middle of the floor. I slowly moved closer and bent over to get a closer look at the single dime staring up at me.

I was relieved to know "I'm on the right path". A healthier one. Emotionally I released visions of the way the marriage had worked for many years. It needed to evolve.

Eventually there were decisions to make in my uncompromising pursuit of healthy living, causing my path to take an unexpected turn. I was an actress in a movie, *my* movie. A documentary featuring my life. And in the role, I had a script to follow; one I had memorized. However, as I acted out the scenes as they unfolded I felt the script and story were different from the one originally written. The life I was living was not the one I was destined for. Internal conflict pushed me out the door and relocated me three hours south to work in a raw food health retreat center in West Palm Beach, Florida. A long-distance marriage was a viable option for a few months, until it was clear I needed to move forward—alone.

I needed to delve deeper and that meant I had to leave my marriage. It was not really a choice. Dean and I were two very different people with conflicting hobbies and interests. I knew I could have one or the other—but not both. The urge to be healthy was intense and undeniable.

The clarity was confirmed during a visit by Dean. I sat in front of him as we sadly faced the reality of divorce. *Were there any stones left unturned? Any solutions not yet thought of?* Before the questions could be answered, his right hand touched his left and spun his silver wedding ring around on his finger. Instantly, the ring broke in half and fell into his right palm.

Shock currents vibrated through the room as we realized what we saw.

A metal ring broke.

Just like that.

"I guess that's that", Dean said.

No further discussion was needed. Dean told me since rings don't normally break he considered it an omen. He understood we had done all we could do together.

I lived by myself, which afforded me absolute control over my home environment. Working at the retreat supplied me with raw vegan food and my body achieved a level of wellness I had known could exist for me. I thought I had finally found it. All the years of suffering led to an actual lifestyle that answered my questions and gave my body what it needed for healing. Gratitude spilled from my being.

I began waking up earlier in the mornings feeling refreshed. Since I had not felt rested in many years, it took some getting used to. When my eyes opened, I felt energy. Yes, I finally felt alive. Popping right out of bed when I woke up was all new to me, no longer did my mind need to coerce my body into moving and functioning.

One morning, it was dark outside yet I was wide awake. Energy stirred within. I turned over onto my back prepared to psych myself out; but I didn't need to. The body underneath the sheets was rearing and ready to dart out of bed and begin the day. I was filled with anticipation: wonder, joy, peace—all the feelings I knew existed in the world. The ones I had searched so desperately for. There was no reason to stay in bed just because it was dark outside; I was rested, revived, and ready for the day!

I floated effortlessly into the kitchen to prepare herbal tea since coffee was not a part of the raw food diet I was sticking stringently to. I awaited the boiling water and wondered what to do. No sooner had the question entered my mind, when it was replaced with a vision of my journal. I spent time writing every day since living on my own and documented the exciting journey. *Of course, I'd write about how great I felt.*

On my way to the bedroom I was halted.

Unable to move.

I stood, entranced, seeing past the double pane sliding doors in the living room.

Even through the ice blue sheer curtain, radiant colors shined though from the sky outside. I gasped at the scene as it enveloped me. Sunrise. Ahhhh, it was the sun rising. *Was it always this amazing? This brilliant?* Quickly I pulled open the sheer curtain, allowing a full panoramic color-fest to fill my senses. A gray backdrop boasted blurred lines filled with bubblegum pink and tangerine orange, scattered around the emerging brilliant golden glow rising slowly on the horizon.

I starred in awe.

The beauty was magical.

God's presence smiled back at me.

Each breath filled my being with the love I saw and felt before me. There was no separation between the energy from the sun, the rainbow of colors filling the sky, the reflection in the pond, and me. The connection was profound. Undeniable. Instead of feeling a sickly body—I finally felt a vibrant life force.

I was wide awake with eyes glued to the mesmerizing beauty. Although I had seen sunrise before, it was never from the viewpoint of a healthy person. The perspective differed as night from day; dark from light. During those moments, I was able to fully release the struggle; all struggles, all stresses. I felt forgiveness within, a cleansing. I was cleansed, purified.

Teardrops lining my cheeks were not from pain, but instead, gratitude; immense gratitude for everything—for the love from God.

Ah, this is what unconditional love feels like!

I savored the slowness of the experience, hoping it would never end. A blinding golden pulsing ball shined light upon the earth around me for the grand finale. I breathed the brilliant sunlight into my body; and again.

I had a great view from my condo, but one morning I wondered what sunrise looked like from the beach. Since I lived on the East coast of Florida, the nearest beach was a mere fifteen-minute drive. I decided to go the next day, knowing it would be even more remarkable.

A blanket and jacket waited for me by the front door as I set my alarm for an ungodly early wake up call. Not knowing how with-it I'd be, I made it easy and all I had to do was grab the stuff and go. Excitedly, I was off to bed.

Sunrise at the beach burst my heart open beyond compare—more than anything I had ever experienced. I continued driving there most mornings and each day filled my body with the loving energy and light. After sunrise I would contemplate, HU, and write poetry on an empty beach. I was thankful others were not aware of the free magical transformation that took place each morning; leaving the sound and light for me alone to enjoy.

One such morning, as the sun shimmered diamonds onto the water before me, I closed my eyes and softly looked at a blank screen behind my third eye, located between the eyebrows and above the nose. I gently sang my favorite spiritual word a few times and relaxed deeper. Suddenly, I caught a glimpse of my future; and it involved a book. *My book.* I zoomed in to the scene to look closely at the book title, *Learning to Love Sunrise,* on the cover.

Learning to Love Sunrise, was clearly about my distaste of mornings during the health challenged years versus the immense love sunrises fill my healthier body with. I knew I was supposed to write about my journey to health. It would be an inspirational story about seeking health and finding even more—inner peace. Who doesn't want that?

I enthusiastically began writing my story and continued journaling.

On a sunny day a few months later, I spoke with an acquaintance seeking a freelance data entry assistant for his latest book. During our discussion, he asked me twice if I had ever done a book. Although I answered the question initially, he asked me the second time. When I answered, *again*, the message came across loud and clear. I heard my reply.

"No, I had not written a book—YET", I repeated.

I was being told I needed to write a book, but it was supposed to be *mine*, not someone else's.

The following month while at dinner with friends, fortune cookies were distributed. I usually joked about the trite sayings inside them. A cookie wrapped in plastic was tossed my way. *Bummer, I didn't even get to choose my own, instead it was given to me. I guess it chose me*, I rationalized.

It read, "You have a charming way with words and should write a book".

Enough said. I wrote, knowing the words would have purpose.

Rewriting My Story

A book did not magically appear. Life got busy and I

continued journaling while it simmered in the background. A change in career, and the opportunity to help others, brought me another step closer, though, even if it was just a warm up.

I pursued my passion for health and studied to became a Certified Nutrition & Wellness Consultant. The role utilized my nutrition, health, and healing experience, along with years of marketing, graphic arts, and customer service skills. There was quite a learning curve when shifting away from the standard American diet, and those seeking health needed an education. I taught about a raw food vegan diet, met for one-on-one consultations, and offered group food preparation classes. I shared an office with another educator in a holistic physician's practice and spent many hours helping patients grasp what they could optimally eat.

Although challenging work, helping people improve their health was emotionally fulfilling. I worked with multiple cancer patients and noticed a repetitive pattern when preparing menus. The same foods needed to be avoided in most every case—none were advised to eat sugar, dairy, gluten, or artificial ingredients. *How could I improve my efficiency and make the information readily available?* Once the question entered my mind, the answer emerged. *I could compile my therapeutic recipes into a booklet.* Instead of individually emailing recipe recommendations to each patient, I could offer them a concise book.

I never thought I would create a recipe book, but that is what happened when I documented my nutrition and health knowledge. In March 2011, I self-printed and spiral bound, *Raw Done Right: food combining and low sugar for health & healing*, which focused on simple, raw, vegan, and gluten free recipes. From a marketing perspective, it was a win-win. It saved me time, repetition of work, *and* created a small income stream.

Years ago, I had the misguided conception that being a spiritually enlightened person meant detaching from worldly things; especially money. Not only detach, but the *less* you had, the better. As if not having funds opened a pipeline directly to God, giving the appearance of being superior based upon willingness to sacrifice. The illusion of worthiness.

Eventually, I realized it was okay to follow my heart and have it repaid financially by the Universe. Money was not the enemy. Since it didn't always happen, I accepted the gift of income with a grateful heart.

I enjoyed my career, but it was not easy work, especially on class days.

I melted into the office chair after a long day, thankful for the opportunity to catch my breath. The last patient had known nothing of the suggested lifestyle and I had started at the beginning with her—the basics. Too bad she could not attend the raw food preparation class I taught that evening, since I covered exactly the same information plus demonstrated how to prepare recipes to sample.

The class was popular; possibly the most helpful tool I offered. The verbal education combined with visual demonstration helped participants learn and retain the information, empowering them to implement changes in their homes; and *that* was the purpose.

It took an hour to set up. I moved the table and each chair, one at a time, from the storage area into the presentation room. Everything else was transported from home. Earlier that morning I had dismantled my kitchen and packed it neatly into several plastic bins. In front of the room I set up the large white folding table and unpacked the large appliances. Two juicers, a VitaMix, food processor, and spiralizer each had their spot on the demonstration table. Raw food gadgets were all lined up in a row. Next the knives, spatulas, garlic press, measuring cups, and spoons were methodically lined up for easy access. They all needed to be within reach while I spoke to the audience and prepared food. Julia Child in training.

On the end of the table I placed plasticware, small

plates, and cups for samples. Everyone loved to taste the recipes after seeing them prepared.

Lastly, I wheeled in the food cooler. It was filled with fresh organic berries, raw cacao powder, spinach, avocados, soaked cashews, garlic, cucumbers, apples, ginger, lemons, flax seeds, and much more raw produce I had shopped for the day before. To keep it all fresh, I did not unpack until class time.

During final preparation, I counted the handouts, verifying I had collated enough for the twenty rsvp's. I handed them out as I greeted participants. I welcomed many new faces who learned about the class from my online marketing campaign, and others I had previously met at raw food events. I was ready for class.

I chose four recipes to demo and sample. First was a green smoothie, because it was always a hit. I liked to start off with a sure thing. After the roar of the VitaMix whipped spinach, berries, avocado, and stevia into a strange creamy blue-green brew, I filled small cups to pass around the room. They sipped the smoothies and let me know they liked the taste much better than the color.

The first half hour I lectured about what raw food was, and was not.

After tantalizing their taste buds, it was time to make a juice. I slowly fed apple, cucumber, kale, beet, and ginger into one of the juicers, separating the juice from the pulp. Some voiced concern that juicing was too time-consuming and overwhelming to implement, so I felt it was important to demonstrate. After taste test number two, I answered many questions about which juicers I recommended and the differences of models. Next on the menu was a creamy pate' of soaked cashews, garlic, lemon, sea salt, and spices blended in the food processor. Sampled on cucumber rounds, most were pleasantly surprised at the ease and taste of the recipe. It was similar to pizza cheese.

I talked the entire time explaining ingredients, use of

gadgets, suggestions for storage, and shopping locations. I also sampled the food myself, enjoying the much-needed energy it contained.

The grand finale was a bit of a splurge. Dessert! I utilized the food processor once again to blend avocado, raw cacao, coconut oil, vanilla, sea salt, and agave into a blissful mousse. If I had not won them over yet—this recipe usually sealed the deal. For those needing to avoid agave, since it was a form of sugar, I explained how to substitute stevia. Everyone could enjoy a little yumminess. And as expected, dessert was the all-star of the evening.

The cooler was empty, every item on the table smeared with food, and most were prepared to make something new at home. Some wanted more recipes and chose to purchase my book. I was thankful I had it to offer. I wrapped up the Q&A and shared my gratitude for their participation. I loved teaching.

Luckily, people helped me put chairs away before they left. Then it was time for serious tear down. With no rhyme or reason, everything was tossed into the plastic bins, table neatly put away, and car loaded. Not done quite yet, though. Once home the bins were unloaded, small items placed in the dishwasher, and appliances hand-washed.

My busy day had finally come to a close—and I was exhausted.

For months, I continued to help others until the energy needed to do the job was more than I had. To my dismay, my health was declining at an alarming rate. It was much harder to encourage dietary and lifestyle changes than originally realized and I was not able to give the support most patients needed for success. I was baffled how someone could gain insightful life-changing information yet not implement it.

I was shown a powerful lesson—not everyone was like *me*. Some were not willing to change what was leading to poor health; even if it was disruptive to their body. Unfortunately, not everyone had strong inner guidance to help keep them on track.

My stringent eating regimen was not enough to keep me healthy while educating others, which posed a personal dilemma. *How could I teach about something that wasn't working for me?* I had to believe in my product. Sadly, I knew my mission was *not* to educate about food. A double hit—my health was spiraling *and* I faced a dead-end career path.

During daily contemplation I asked for guidance, feeling confident my life was off-track. I was confused, conflicted, and actively seeking my purpose. Although I had completed a book, it did not make my heart sing. It was time to search deeper. *Was there something else I was supposed to do?*

My philosophy of "being actively present and living in the moment" was kicked up a few notches, as I paid close attention for signs to guide me toward my higher calling. My passion. Whatever I was meant to do in this lifetime.

Within a few months, I was offered an opportunity to attend a ten-day raw food program at Living Foods Institute in Atlanta, Georgia. Excitement, at last! Although I was contemplating a new career direction no longer revolving around food, I welcomed the healthy environment for quality, private, and overdue writing time. A place to focus without distraction.

No flight, just an easy drive from Florida to Atlanta. I enjoyed road trips and confidently made my way north after all details fell perfectly into place. Another thing to be grateful for—the ability to recognize a power higher than myself involved in trip planning. When all goes well, don't interfere—just go along for the ride.

The program filled the daytime hours surrounding me with thirty-some eager attendees. The mornings were spent in the kitchen learning food preparation. Most were new to the lifestyle and excited for the amazing hands-on opportunity. How better to learn than to prepare your own lunch? I knew first-hand about food preparation and all it entailed, so I appreciated the opportunity to sit back. After-all, I was seeking a quiet writing retreat *outside* of the kitchen.

We arranged our own accommodations and would part ways come dinner time. I had made reservations at a different hotel after being awoken at 2:00 am by cigarette smoke from the adjoining room the first night. I was hopeful my next choice would be more suitable.

A passionate speaker, Jake, was part of the program that day. I noticed his infectious energy as we spoke one-on-one in the afternoon. Somehow, he had heard of my "smoky room" dilemma and insisted I meet Gail Lash. She was a therapist on staff and rented a few rooms in her home to program participants. I sensed a fond connection the moment I met her and cancelled the hotel reservation.

Anticipation vibrated through me as I turned into the driveway of her home. *Why was I nervous?* I took a few deep breaths before making my way across the driveway onto the wrap around porch. To my left I spotted a huge labyrinth made with small stones consuming the front yard. It was breath-taking. I couldn't look away. My eyes located the starting point along the outside perimeter and slowly followed the path around, and around. It was a tranquil moment as I imagined my body slowly moving along the path, eventually stepping into the middle.

That instant, mentally walking into the middle of the labyrinth, was pivotal. I moved away from my previous careers and *toward* becoming a writer.

I saw a peace pole standing in the yard. I had seen my first one a couple years earlier while working at a raw food retreat in Patagonia, Arizona. It was very fitting there because the location was truly the most peaceful place I had ever experienced.

The World Peace Prayer Society describes a Peace Pole as an internationally-recognized symbol of the hopes and dreams of humans. Each bears the message—May Peace Prevail on Earth—in different languages on each of its four or six sides. There are tens of thousands of Peace Poles in nearly every country in the world dedicated as monuments to peace.

What does a Peace Pole mean to me? It represents love; love and inner peace. Peace within. The pole reads, May Peace Prevail On Earth. I would rewrite mine to say, May Peace Prevail Within.

I stood, entranced by the peaceful symbol, knowing I had arrived at the right place.

I was fortunate to rent a room in a beautiful historic two-story 1894 Victorian home. Inside, it rivaled a museum. Each room I walked past offered glimpses into other lands. I made my way up the curved wooden stairway leading to the second level. My eyes were distracted by a plethora of ornate decorations, pictures, and tapestries filling the walls. Being a simplistic person, it seemed visually similar to standing in New York at Times Square for the first time.

Two bedrooms and a bathroom lined each side of the hallway, which then opened into a massive open area. Home offices were tucked into the left side just past my room, and a recreational area utilized the remaining space. It must have taken half a forest to create the original wooden floors stretched before me.

The homeowners were a delightful couple. They had traveled the world together and peace was definitely their theme. One organization they were involved with promoted peace via tourism. Their home was filled with treasures and trinkets from around the world; exotic locations foreign to me. I knew nothing about distant lands or other cultures. During enlightening discussions, they shared differences and similarities between people, no matter where they were on the earth. My new friends believed in the connectedness of all things. All life. All people being the same.

After returning from dinner one evening I joined them, Jake, and a few visitors in the living area downstairs. The room was filled with dynamic energy and conversation. That night I needed the energy. Not physically—but mentally. My world expanded as I became immersed in the exchange.

I had not talked much about myself—I was in *listening* mode.

Eventually the discussion moved in a more personal direction, aiming a spotlight my way.

"Tell us about *your* path, Pam", Gail inquired.

I straightened my posture in the corner seat of the sofa, then spoke of my journey, experiences, lessons, spiritual beliefs, and writing. All the things that led me to the exact place I was sitting: on the sofa, in their home, at that exact moment. The perfect alignment of life; especially when it was not in my control.

While sharing raw food and health knowledge, I was nudged to share my booklet. We talked on and on but the image of the book cover would not disappear from my consciousness. Everyone was chiming in on the lively topic, so I took the opportunity to step away briefly to retrieve one from my car.

The divine guidance did not ask me to walk back in and brag about my tiny little booklet. Instead, I spotted Gail in the hallway near the kitchen entrance and knew *she* was the one I was to share it with. I joined her, happy for a moment alone.

"I want to share something with you", I said. "I have a small raw food recipe book I wrote to help me with my consultations. For some reason, I feel a nudge to share it with you."

Nervous fingers placed it into her hands.

She looked briefly at the front, turned it over, and read the author write up on the back cover.

When done, she affectionately looked into my eyes.

"This is your story. Are you willing to rewrite it?", she asked.

The world stopped for a moment—refused to spin. *What?* That was not the response I was expecting.

Thoughts spun around my head. *What did she see? What*

did she know? And what did she just say? Are you willing to rewrite it? If I rewrote my story, what would it say? As I connected with the moving planet again, it was obvious she did not think the book fulfilled my purpose any more than I did.

Before bed I journaled her precise words because I knew they were significant, even though I was puzzled of their meaning.

The liveliness of the day program vied for my headspace, attempting to keep my personal answers from surfacing. If information kept entering my mind, it would never be empty enough for guidance to speak. There would be no space for it to land. I would not hear it. I needed to balance attending the final days of the program with writing time, to maintain my spiritual connection.

I woke up the morning after I heard Gail's message and chose to partake in a silent day. That entailed refraining from talking to *anyone* unless it was *absolutely* necessary. While not talking, the ability to listen was heightened.

What do you hear when you are not talking? When you are not thinking about what you are going to say? Or, how you are going to respond? I placed a name tag on my shirt that read, "I'm having a silent day". After all, I did not want anyone to think I was ignoring them.

Since I was not vocalizing words in conversation, I was moved to pen my thoughts to paper. I located a peaceful floor space in a corner between treatment rooms and began writing in my journal. Admiring the rays of sunshine and bamboo trees swaying in the breeze through a large picture window, I started by writing a few poems. After the words were scrawled onto the page, I read them. Then read them again. I felt immense gratification maneuvering words to express emotions into poetic melody.

When done, I reflected on the process. *My* process. *How did I write a poem? Where did the words come from?* Then I thought about journaling. *If I'm journaling and I have a question, how do I ask to receive an answer?*

I booted up my laptop and spent hours typing pages of details on how to contemplate and journal to obtain answers. I wrote the techniques I used and gave several examples. The excitement was building! I saw a book unfolding before me. One that would help people find their own answers, just as I had learned to find mine—by writing.

The following morning we met in the classroom, formed a large circle with chairs, and spent time learning about the power of positive thoughts. As a homework assignment, each of us was to come up with a personal affirmation written in the present tense—as if we had already achieved it. Instantly, my left hand picked up the pen and wrote on the notecard, "I am a successful, happy, joyful, healthy, prosperous, artist, writer, and educator. I teach about journaling, writing, and poetry."

I saw a vision of teaching about the power of journaling.

On the seventh day of the program, I spent the entire day at the house writing. The home held so many nooks and crannies to nestle in to cozily write, but I was drawn to stay in my room since it afforded the most privacy. I knew to allow my heart to fully open, it was paramount to surround myself with safe space and positive energy. My connection to Spirit, God, or a higher power, was stronger than ever and words were pouring through. I had come on the trip seeking a spiritual connection and knew writing was most important. My heart was wide open shining love onto my written pages.

Unforeseen crossroads were approaching, leading to multiple life-changing decisions. Listening had become one of my most valuable spiritual tools. The ability to calm the mind and let it know it did not have all the answers; nor need to.

I heard:

my body tell me it couldn't keep up with my chosen profession, the idea to write a recipe book,

the speaker, Jake, suggest I stay at Gail's house,

the insight of rewriting my story—an important message on my "silent day" of listening,

the divine love of God sprinkle inner guidance.

I heard all those things. The more experiences I recognized, the more I craved silence.

And peace.

Peace. That is what I sought when I traveled to Arizona years before, walked my first labyrinth, and witnessed the emotional charge within a Peace Pole. In Georgia, the important symbol stood again by another labyrinth, as I shifted to become a writer. And ironically, I see a Peace Pole every day when I look out the window of my home office in Florida. Across the street, under a bottlebrush tree sit two midnight blue Adirondack chairs—facing a lovely white Peace Pole.

Gail's words planted a seed and set in motion a revision to my story. The wheels were turning for my next writing project and possible career path. I was led one step closer to the book you hold in your hands. The other two visions of books still simmer in the background, waiting to move forward when the time is right. Will they be completed? Are they meant to be? Or was the *Learning to Love Sunrise* vision to keep me journaling about my life and the signs I was following? Was *Journal for Your Own Answers* a reminder of how I needed to continue asking, seeking, and listening in my own life? Time will tell.

Meanwhile, I was rewriting my story. And listening. Tuning in ever deeper to hear my truth. It is a good thing I became a better listener, because a life-changing message was just around the corner.

5

LIFE-CHANGING INNER MESSAGE

What am I here to do?

*S*ometimes a private message is communicated or a vision seen on our inner screen to provide guidance into our life. The interpretation might be undeniable. Other times, only a subtle nudge is given to assist in moving us along toward a destination that is unclear or uncertain. It may take months, or even years, to piece together signs we recognized at the time that dramatically influenced us to take a chance, follow a nudge, pursue a passion, or conquer a fear—to live the life we have intended for ourselves. In reflection, clues always guided the way.

In May 2012, during a spiritual contemplation, I heard one of the undeniable messages pointing me toward my purpose. The words were clear, but my mission was not—at first.

The room was serene. Butterscotch walls were elegantly adorned with large thin colorfully painted cloths while lamps strategically placed in two corners set the appropriate ambiance for Yoga. A shrine with Buddha figurines was displayed in another corner.

I was thankful for the final relaxing pose called Savasana, and thankful for the end of class. The restorative pose supplied my body and mind much needed rest. I reflected on my three-month struggle while attempting to complete a Yoga Teacher Training Certification. I relaxed deeper with each inhalation. I was never convinced becoming an instructor was the path for me, but it seemed something I needed to try. I thought it would be an opportune way to earn a living and keep my body healthy at the same time.

The certification program lasted nearly a year and classes met one weekend a month—on Friday evening, all day Saturday, and all day Sunday. In between sessions, time was filled with attending various yoga classes at the studio and studying the written materials that included ten books ranging in topics from yoga poses, the muscular skeletal system, and spiritual philosophy. I was a bit trepidatious but thought it was something I could complete.

I was excited for the first class to begin. I was *still* excited during the first hour of class. But after that, the reality of the physical demands and mental faculties needed began to present themselves. By Sunday of the first weekend, I knew I needed to reevaluate. Although I spoke with the teacher about my concerns, she was clueless how challenging it was. No one understood the pain and throbbing my muscles endured as they tried to figure out what to do—and what I was doing *to* them.

Just twelve hours prior, while at home singing HU, I had desperately asked on the inner for help. Guidance. Wisdom. Whatever I needed to know to ease my pain. Since I am not one to ask for help, I realized I was in a state of total distress.

Since the deep throbbing impacted my legs, I wondered if it was a clue.

Still singing, I posed a question.

"Am I walking the right path, or is this the *wrong* path and that's why it's my legs that are compromised?", I had asked.

I patiently waited. No response. Nothing.

I knew I had been slacking on my spiritual exercises by not singing HU each day or reading spiritual books. My connection to God, or Spirit, was not as strong without the daily practice. A friend of mine recently said, "I have a conflict with church and another event Thursday night. No decision, God wins!"

I knew that God needed to always win in my life, too!

The soothing scent of lavender brought me back to the present moment.

The end of class.

Somehow, I had made it to Saturday morning of the third month and was lying on my back, arms and legs spread at 45 degrees, eyes closed, and breathing deep. Savasana, also referred to as Corpse pose, is said to be extremely challenging because there is an art to remaining consciously alert while still being at ease. Being still was my forte. The asana, meaning pose, was not as challenging as the physical ones for me thanks to the many years I had practiced spiritual contemplative exercises. Contemplation differs from meditation. Meditation is passive, like standing in front of a door waiting for it to open. Contemplation, however, is more active—visualize opening the door and walking through it.

I loved that part of class. It was quiet with no instructions, no talking. Very peaceful.

Lovely flute music meandered softly through the still yet vibrant air we continued filling our lungs with. A hint of diffused essential oil helped soothe, refresh, and balance. I was not aware of twenty-five people in the room, instead I was enveloped in my own private world.

The warm room cocooned my ailing physical body, melting each muscle deeper into the soft yoga mat.

I tuned-in to the body surrounding me that needed to function on this plane of existence, and wondered why I'm here. I pondered how to phrase the statement before placing it in my consciousness for guidance. Sometimes it's how a question is asked that dictates if an answer will present itself. If a blank inner screen remains after several minutes, I might reword the inquiry in hopes of obtaining a response.

My heart was open, full of love, and ready to learn about

my next step.

As I lightly focused on the glowing cobalt blue light expanding to fill my third eye, even more love flowed. I tried to contain the tears bubbling up.

I inquired as simply as possible.

"What am I here to do?", I slowly asked inwardly.

I inhaled deeply.

The response was instantaneous.

"To speak", a voice began.

"To teach", it continued.

"To speak of God", it said.

I was still.

In a state of shock.

Dumbfounded.

To speak of God?

I grappled to comprehend.

The response was irrefutable. Very clear words were relayed but no vision of what it looked like within the confines of my life. I was confident more guidance would follow and I needed to keep my heart open to receive it. Still in a semiconscious state, I wanted to know more about my mission and how to keep the inner connection alive to help guide me. Questions flooded my mind.

"How do I stay connected?", I further inquired.

Only a few seconds elapsed before I heard the answer.

"At the water", the voice suggested.

During the final moments of class, I relished in my peaceful inner experience as warm salty tears trickled along my cheekbone; no longer held inside, they flowed freely.

I had asked a question and received a life-changing answer. *My* answer. I did not know how I would "speak of God" quite yet, but clearly needed to continue my beach walks to stay connected and open to my inner guidance.

I could have stayed in that happy place for hours, but it was time to return to my physical body—and the physical plane world. The class was over and I had two hours before the afternoon session began. But Saturday afternoon, during the lunch break, I knew I should push no more. I left the studio for lunch and never returned. Heart broken, I left a message for the teacher to withdraw. I knew I was to walk a different road.

Although I did not complete the training program, it was there I received a most important message illuminating my path. I was journaling and participating in more spiritual events, which was setting the groundwork. We are not ready for all the pieces and answers to come at once—they build on each other. Our consciousness opens up one level at a time. It is similar to a building that begins with a strong foundation, then the walls are erected, a second level added, and topped off with a roof. My strong foundation included daily HU songs and spiritual exercises.

Four years after I received the message, I was editing this story and preparing to speak at a worship service on the theme of creativity and gratitude. While pondering on the topic, I had a profound realization.

I was speaking of God.

What a powerful ah-ha moment! Gratitude spilled like a waterfall as my purpose was finally clear. My mission was love. Gratitude. Service. And I would finally get to utilize my creativity. Exciting times lie ahead, indeed.

But first, I needed to wrap up a pesky health challenge. With the foundation laid, my consciousness opened ever so slightly, enabling me to spend the following year learning more about what the ailment had to teach me. If I learned the lesson, I could move on. Onto this path where I speak of God.

6

GIFT OF HEALING

A Time for Healing

My listening skills were improving, allowing me to gain trust in my intuition and nudges. I was learning to ask questions and listen for guidance. One thing I had difficulty with, however, was asking for help. I figured if something was in my life then I needed to deal with it. Figure out the meaning. I never realized asking for help was even an option. That is, until I reached a breaking point. A rock bottom. A moment of desperation. And on that day, while filled with anguish and frustration, I cried out for help—not expecting such an extraordinary response.

On a spring-like Friday afternoon less than a year after hearing about why I'm here—to speak of God—I was on my way to one of my favorite regional spiritual seminars. Road trips were enjoyable. I could play any music I chose, sing along, or savor the quiet time. That day, I craved the silence.

Golden sunshine paved the road I travelled from south Florida to Orlando. I reminisced of previous seminars I had attended and was ready for another uplifting event.

A throbbing headache accompanied me on the drive. I had struggled mightily with health issues for too many years. Although only in my mid-forties, for eighteen years I had battled severe exhaustion, food intolerances, headaches, muscle fatigue, unbalanced hormones, and depression.

Recently menopause symptoms were added to the mix. In reality, I never felt good. Even though I was looking forward to the retreat, sadness overwhelmed me. I was extremely frustrated with the ongoing health situation and confused about my employment outlook because of it.

Really, is this why I'm here? To spend all this time and effort on food? On health stuff? Changing what I eat every two months?

My head was reeling.

Each day was spent mustering up energy to move my body. I had to figure out a game plan since I had become my own doctor years before. Little known to my friends, I was working on my doctorate degree in figuring-out-health-on-this-planet. *What should I eat? Should I juice vegetables? Blend food into a smoothie? Eat all raw? Vegan? Paleo? Exercise by walking? Yoga? Weight lifting? Or avoid it all because recovery was too challenging?* Yes, my head was spinning—no wonder it was throbbing.

I just wanted to live without so much effort. To awaken and rise to meet the day with a smile, instead of tears. To feel like I belong on this earth, instead of wondering why I was placed on the wrong planet. To live a life of joy and peace. *Was there any peace for me?* I thought there must be because my inner drive was so strong—as if it knew what it was striving for.

I recall that peaceful and joyful feeling—but it was not from my current time on earth.

I participated in a past life regression a few years before because I wondered if there was a reason for the relentless struggles with my body this time around. During the hypnosis, I witnessed myself in a recent lifetime serving as a healer of sorts. The deep love for my chosen profession filled me with peace, joy, and contentment. It was my purpose. However, as I released ailments from suffering Souls the karma landed upon my slate. Although my efforts were pure in nature and heart, the result was the same—the karma was set free and it had to go somewhere. And now, during my current incarnation, I was forced to endure the suffering I had mistakenly released.

The understanding gained from the enlightening experience also helped me grasp the reason for my hesitation to give advice to others. I believe only *they* know their course, the one they chose to come here and learn from. It is not my place to direct anyone in any direction and I feel I have intruded on their personal space if I inadvertently made a suggestion. Admittedly, I was drawn to helping people with health, just as I had done as the healer—but a loving guide seemed to be directing me toward another path. So, I guess the good news is I am not repeating the same mistake this time around!

Understanding where some of the challenge came from was extremely helpful, but I was not healed by the information and was at my wit's end.

My ultimate desire was to use my creative graphic arts and writing skills. *Why else would I have them?* A healthy body and mind were integral pieces to successfully tap into creative space, I knew I needed my body and mind aligned.

As I neared the exit, I focused on the dazzling sunlight leading my way.

I arrived at the hotel, checked-in, and trudged my luggage up to the room. Somehow, I successfully unpacked before all remaining energy abandoned my body. I collapsed onto the bed, grasping for pillows to squeeze feverishly for comfort. Filled with overwhelming despair, tears broke through the wall I had built. The wall I wanted to hold them inside. As long as they were contained, I could keep my composure and seem strong on the outside. But I was not strong at that moment. I was weak. And I was desperate. A volcano of frustration erupted as I trembled in agony. I needed help.

I knew I had done all I could do and needed to seek higher guidance. I decided to do a spiritual exercise and ask for help.

Outstretched on the bed, I began to breathe. Then deeper still, relaxing with each inhale. I closed my eyes. After a few minutes the tears stopped flowing and dried on my face. I was no longer putting attention on how I felt, but instead began pleading for help.

"Can I be finished with the food and health challenges? Please let me know what I need to do so I can be done and move on. Help me, please. I have so much I feel I can create and offer in this lifetime. How can I earn a living, have enough energy, and be creative?", internally I begged.

Stillness filled my body as the breathing penetrated deeper. Although there was not enough energy to sing aloud, I sang HU to God internally. I tried to keep an open and empty mind so an answer would have a place to fall into.

When I opened my eyes twenty minutes later, I was confident I would receive clarity regarding my plea sometime during the weekend seminar.

Filled with confidence, I surmised I no longer needed to figure out my health. I would simply be open and aware of signs pointing toward my answer. A sense of relief filled my body—somehow relaxed yet energetic. My cells had awakened. Thankful for the life force, I hurried to ready myself for the evening program and was on my way downstairs without further thought about my question, plea, or inner feeling I had gained.

I sat with a friend during the program and enjoyed a lengthy chat afterwards. Not wanting to break up the party, I offered to share my hotel room. She considered the gesture since her room was quite full, but had difficulty deciding. We parted ways and I let her know she was welcome to join me anytime before 10:00 pm.

After saying goodnight, I knew either way would be fine. I could have a roommate, or my own space. I had no attachment to either outcome but instead was open to whichever experience I needed. As I sat in bed journaling about my day, I knew it was too late for her to join me and I would have my own space for the retreat.

My limited diet dictated I eat certain foods that were not always available in restaurants. Even though I brought what I needed with me, when I woke up I felt a strong undeniable pull to dine downstairs. I did not question the nudge, instead I looked forward to having a nice warm breakfast prepared for me.

I was waiting at the omelet station and caught the eye of a man also attending the seminar. I recognized him but we had never spoken. As the chef handed me my plate, the man looked it over.

"Are you a vegetarian?", he inquired.

My eyes smiled back at him.

I took a deep breath and pondered my response.

"You know, I've been sick for many years and I'll do whatever I need to do to get well", was my reply.

"I don't think I could be a vegetarian," he stated.

"Well, I don't want to go into any details. I'll just say I'm frustrated because I have to change what I eat every two to three months due to severe food reactions," I shared.

Holding my emotions back I added, "Last night during my contemplation I asked to be shown an answer so I could be done with it!"

He showed concern and asked me a few questions about the food and reactions. I kept my answers brief.

In less than sixty seconds the words, "It sounds to me like leaky gut syndrome", rolled off his tongue.

I had never heard of leaky gut. *What was this health condition?*

We talked a few minutes longer and I learned he was a retired chiropractor, educator, and author. His name was Dr. Jason Schwartz—a man with experience in what *I* was having difficulty with. How fortunate.

I returned to my table squeezing tear-filled eyes. Sadness was not pushing them out this time, it was excitement.

Was this the answer I'd asked for last night?
Was it the answer I'd searched eighteen years for?

I was emotional, grateful, and hopeful as I let the moment sink in.

I ate breakfast in a stupor then hurried to my room to research leaky gut on the computer. I was blown away at the parallel of the symptoms listed in relation to my illness progression through the years. I learned that no matter what diet I ate, even the healthiest organic food, it would only work for a couple months—until my body got "used to it" and started treating it like a toxin. Oh my, it finally made sense.

Yes, indeed, it was my answer.

I finally knew *what* I was dealing with.

My search for an answer was finally over and the healing process could begin. What a blessing!

My plea had been answered.

I was guided in so many ways on that magical weekend. By not being attached to an outcome, either having a roommate or not, I was given private space in order to feel the nudge to go to the restaurant. It was there the spiritual importance of listening was clearly demonstrated once again. The added lesson of learning to ask—for help, guidance, or assistance—was profound. Literally life-changing.

Within six months of hearing my answer, I completed a nutritional protocol which allowed my body to finally mend after eighteen years. During a spiritual exercise, I later learned the first ten years balanced the karma from my lifetime as a healer, and the remaining eight I had brought on myself during my 20's when I totally neglected my body.

The healing I had worked so hard for was just in the nick of time—because unknowingly, I had a special appointment at a spiritual seminar in Minneapolis just two short weeks later.

Part III: Jeff

Jeff & Pam Terrell

7

GROWING UP JEFF

Many Realities

An Open Creative Mind

I was a happy and fortunate child. Sure, I had my struggles—we all do—but I also had moments of absolute peace, contentment, and clarity of being. Looking back, I can recognize that Spirit was working in my life in many ways. Experiences demonstrated that the totality of life's lessons cannot always be fully appreciated when the poignant events originally occur. Sometimes, the value of the perspective time provides, coupled with an opened heart, reveals wonderful gifts.

The earth seemed much bigger when I was young. My perception of the physical environment, as well as worldview, was driven by day to day experiences. My mother never learned to drive a car; she did not need to because she did not have a job outside our home. My father was a doctor in high demand who worked late hours to provide for his family. Without dad around to shuttle us we were left with only one mode of transportation—our feet. So, we walked, everywhere.

It did not take long for me to develop a deep love of walking. It was a state of being, not simply a means of getting from point A to point B. There was something magically uplifting about moving through the landscape which provided fertile ground for some of my best thinking, problem solving, and reflecting. Steve Jobs, the genius behind the Apple computer and the iPhone, was famous for holding important meetings with people while out on a stroll. I may have been young, but I was on to something.

In many respects, however, walking has become a lost art. Now-a-days people tend to be in a hurry to get somewhere other than where they are. In doing so, consciousness is projected out of the present moment and instead, placed into some future event or location. Walking combines these two states, allowing one to be present in the moment, while still moving through space with the change of scenery and input it provides.

The downside of traveling by foot, however, was that I could not get very far on this huge planet. At the time, I thought I was walking to the ends of the earth. But as an adult with a car at my disposal, I recall looking at a map showing a dot labeled with the name of a small town only four miles from my home of eighteen years—and I had never heard of it. I figured that was because there was never a reason to go there.

Imagination was at my disposal, as it is with most children. It was a special time, before being taught to disregard experiences in favor of hardcore "reality". It was totally natural for me to explore other worlds simultaneously with this physical one. They blended together seamlessly. So much so, in fact, I did not even notice the difference. Dreams at night were cut of the same cloth—they were just as real.

Can you imagine what things would be like today if children's multi-dimensional adventures were encouraged and accepted as reality by adults? Picture yourself discussing their dreams at the breakfast table, treating them as real. "Imaginary" friends would be accepted also. Adults might be reminded of these realities, which could help them explore their own dreams in order to gain greater understanding of their lives in the expanded state of consciousness this multi-dimensional approach provides. The exuberance and enchantment of the child could inspire adults to dream even bigger dreams.

Many would argue that to encourage such an attitude would produce a generation of children not properly grounded in reality. If your focus was strictly on this physical plane, then yes, reality might suffer. Sure, we need to have our feet on the ground to properly function in this earthly realm.

Math, science, and structured teachings do have their place. But if we were to also encourage the creative imagination in earnest, the blending of these disciplines could produce well-rounded individuals, permanently plugged in to the higher states of consciousness. It is in these elevated states where real answers to the problems that plague individuals are found. I realize that is kind of a paradox—the real answers we need to solve life's problems down here actually come from above, or within.

Toys, along with an innate imaginative ability, were my tools of transportation into other worlds where anything was possible. Daydreams came alive as my creations catapulted my mind to dream bigger. Always bigger.

Using my basic metal erector set, for instance, I created the highest towers the world had ever seen. These magnificent skyscrapers were built by workers using massive trucks and tractors able to move so much soil and rock that they reshaped the surface of the earth. My five-foot square sandbox in the backyard was, at times, the size of an entire state. In it, I constructed gargantuan dams to hold back mighty rivers. The machines and tools I used fueled my imagination and brought me into the worlds I created. Everything there would spin and move in symmetry and perfection. It was my world.

While in build-mode, nothing could penetrate the solid sphere I resided in. An entire day would pass before I knew it. My mother tried calling me in for supper as she did with my brothers, but resorted to yelling my name repetitively to capture my attention. If I was in the basement playing, she would eventually come downstairs to find me totally engrossed in an alternative world.

My creative mind was more than a tool to keep me occupied while living in a small town. Instead, it was a portal projecting my state of consciousness into "real" worlds—ones I created from my imagination. Yes, these realms were as real as the physical one my body lived in.

I grew up in a modest three-bedroom home in a suburban neighborhood with my parents and two brothers. Three boys with only two bedrooms meant that two of us had to share. Since I was the middle child, I ended up being the one doing the sharing. My little brother had his own room, the nursery, and I bunked with my big brother until he became a teenager. He then got his own space, the former nursery, and my little bro moved in with me. I was okay either way because it was nice having someone to talk with after lights out.

I slept in a drawer. My bed was a trundle; practical for a small room. Before I went to sleep each night, I bent down and hauled the heavy oak drawer out from under my brother's bed. One good thing about sleeping in a drawer was not having to make the bed in the morning. I just shoved it back in and everything was tidy and hidden away.

The imagination utilized during the day also served me well at night. Dreams were not limited to the construction of giant towers. Night dreams propelled me into experiences in universes that exist at higher vibratory rates than the physical.

I recall one night when these higher worlds—those normally outside the visible spectrum—made themselves known to me. I lay awake staring blankly at the ceiling in the dimly lit room I shared with my older brother. He was away spending the night with his friend, and that meant I got to have my friend, Alan, sleep over at my house. We had talked awhile until he fell asleep—leaving me wide awake.

I sensed movement in my peripheral vision and quickly looked left.

Before me stood a semi-transparent form of Alan. It was dressed in pajamas standing on my brother's bed with his head nearly touching the ceiling. The figure was translucent—weightless—as it hovered.

Interestingly, the sound of light snoring let me know Alan was asleep. I glanced up at the bed, and sure enough, a large lump underneath the blanket confirmed his physical body was indeed sleeping.

I blinked hard, as if to clear the image. But when I looked up again, I saw the same mystical vision.

Enthralled by the ghostly form, I watched and waited. Within seconds, the sheer image silently turned around and fell slowly—ever so slowly—backwards, landing gracefully on the lump in bed. At that moment, it was reunited with its physical body.

I watched him stir and roll over in bed.

What just happened?

My eyes travelled back and forth between where the apparition hovered seconds before and Alan's sleeping body under the covers. I had never seen anything like that!

The experience did not originate in this world, but for some reason I was not scared in the least. I had often witnessed friends in the same shadowy form visit me on sleepless nights. They were not nightmares, I was sure—I was wide awake.

Another night that same summer, I awoke at 2:00 am and saw my friend, Julie, standing beside my bed. We had begun a conversation in a dream, and after I awakened in the physical body we were able to continue the dialog for several more minutes. I hardly knew the difference between that visit or seeing her on the neighborhood street. When the conversation was over, her image faded into the soft shadows.

I gazed up at the eerie ceiling reflecting upon the talk we could have. I felt closer to Julie after the experience. Since the boys hung out together and the girls played separately, there was seldom an opportunity for us to speak. Perhaps, that is why the discussion happened in that private way.

Those experiences showed me that while our bodies sleep, we are certainly not asleep. We leave the physical shell behind and allow it to rest while continuing to live lives in other universes. These places do exist and are as solid to us while in the dream, as this world seems to us while we are awake. When we return upon awakening, we recall certain "memories" from these other worlds; we call these memories, dreams.

Lights

Winter in northwestern Pennsylvania sometimes hung on well into spring. Although summer did eventually arrive, it snuck up without notice. One day would be cold, dreary, and windy—then the next was hot and steamy. I loved long summer days that seemed to go on without end. I got up each morning with the sun, played all day, and still saw light in the sky at bedtime.

When the sun finally did go down, the fireflies took over to light up the night. The world was so alive. The sounds through the open window were softer than in winter and filled my ears while lying in bed. Everything sounded better—the crickets, cars passing by, and curtains rustling. The wonderful smells of freshly cut grass in the daytime and musky night air filled my senses.

The connection with my inner life was enhanced as well when the skin on my bare feet connected with the cool earth on those warm days. It was during one of my walks when I was ten years old that a wondrous event occurred, forever changing the way I looked at my formerly small world on a huge planet.

Our home was on the corner in a small subdivision. The

neighborhood was filled with plenty of kids and something was always going on.

In contrast to the non-stop activity, directly across the street loomed a deep dark forest. I looked out our living room window imagining the shady cool trees spread out into uncharted reaches of the world. On that hot afternoon, the coolness of the forest called to me. I decided I would explore them by myself—alone. The shadowy breeze was luring me in, offering a cool and peaceful experience.

I slipped on my shoes and socks, hurried out the door, and before I knew it had reached the end of my driveway. Slight hesitation surfaced as I looked to my left, then right, before crossing the dividing street. The main road; the one separating my playful surroundings from the unknown awaiting me on the other side.

Filled with anticipation, I cautiously crossed the street setting my red ball jet shoes upon the pathway mom had shown me. I summoned the courage to venture in and probe deeper than I had with her and my brothers.

Beneath my feet was a double-track, two dirt tire ruts with tall green grass in between, stretching as far as I could see. About a hundred yards in, they went up over a small rise and then almost imperceptibly, turned right, disappearing into the dark shadows of the trees. I analyzed the tracks. Although the ruts were free of greenery, it did not look as though anyone had driven there recently because the weeds in between were fresh, tall, and undisturbed. I wanted to make sure no one had gone in that day because I did not want any surprises.

I put one foot in front of the other wading into the opening. Nervously, I glanced around admiring the ageless trees surrounding me. They were much taller than the maples dad planted on the side of our house.

Once at the top of the little rise, I gazed into the gloom. My eyes reached into the woods to see what lie ahead. A mysterious gray form stared back, squatting underneath the forest canopy. It appeared to be the destination for the double-track.

Should I go further?

I didn't see a car or any lights. There was hushed silence with only the soft sound of the wind in the trees to meet my ears.

I continued on. The gray square slowly morphed into a structure I recognized—a small, and very old, cabin. It appeared to be deserted. The roof, green with moss, blended into the forest canopy. The gray unpainted board siding sagged off its tired frame, with several missing pieces. A makeshift door, which looked like an afterthought, had been painted a cheerful red at one time. Now worn and faded, separated from the hinges and no longer fitting into the door frame, was nailed in place. Old newspaper covered the only window in the door.

I looked for signs someone was there, or had been in the last decade. To my right I saw where the double-track faded, blending into what used to be a small yard. I walked over. No trees, only grass buried my feet. Standing in the pure silence a few moments, I concluded it was just an abandoned old shack. I wondered what else was hiding in the forest.

My eyes, aided by the small clearing of the "yard" and having adjusted to the dark of the forest, spotted a metal object sticking out of the ground. Emboldened, I marched to the corner of the yard, stopping in front of a well with an old-fashioned hand pump. Unable to resist, my small hand grabbed the rusty handle and lifted it. To my surprise, it moved. It creaked and moaned, but was not rusted shut. I figured it would take quite a few pumps to pull water deep in the ground up to the surface.

Sadly, after a few minutes of pushing and pulling the metal handle, I knew there would be no water. That must be why the old place had been abandoned so long ago, I theorized—the well had gone dry.

Wiping rusty hands onto my shorts, I noticed the forest

fell silent again.

Behind the cabin, pine needles marked the edge of unexplored terrain revealing nothing but pine trees. As far as I knew, no one had ever gone further into the woods than the point where I stood.

It was cool and airy, even in the heat of summer. A forbidding layer of needles crunched under each step, preventing any growth beneath them. The towering trees enveloped my small frame and sunlight barely penetrated the thick craggy branches. In fact, only the smallest flecks of light snuck past the boughs to shine onto the forest floor. The evergreens were in control of the forest, both up and down.

Were there any animals here? I certainly did not hear any. Glancing skyward checking for birds, only the wind whispered through the tree tops. The uppermost branches softly swayed in the warm breeze.

It seemed even a gale-force wind could not have penetrated the closed off world the pines held sway over. The top of the forest shielded against elements from above, but it also blocked light and warmth. *Perhaps that's the real reason the cabin lay abandoned*, I surmised.

Through a crack in the evergreen canopy, I saw into the deep blue world above. It reached out to me—speaking a familiar language. I understood the call from the whispering wind as it gently pulled my awareness out of the darkness and into the nest of the upper limbs. From that vantage point, I admired the unlimited expanse of the powder blue sky.

Although I was outside in the forest where I had been summoned to, it did not feel quite right. Above I saw the vast blue and knew something waited for me elsewhere.

I needed the light—more light.

My mind jolted into action, recalling that the path leading into the forest paralleled a sweeping meadow. The open space would be an inviting change from the dark protected place I stood.

I doubled back, crunching over the pine needle carpet to arrive on the path by the cabin. Trekking out of the deepest part of the woods, my spirits lifted. With a new spring in my step, I bound along by the stand of trees linking the double-track to the perimeter of the meadow. I ducked between limbs to arrive in the corner of the expanse. Stalks of wheat along the edge were broken and short; like the grass in the yard at the cabin.

As I pushed forward into the open space the blades grew taller, nearly to my shoulders. I glided forward with my arms out to my sides hip height, fingers spread wide. Lovingly stroking the blades in response, I drifted aimlessly into the sea of wheat. The meadow welcomed me as I turned my gaze upward again, absorbing the warm caress of the summer sun upon my face. It was a stunning contrast from the way the pine forest had closed me in under its cool and forbidding grasp.

A deep breath of its sweet aroma propelled me in a bit further, to where I believed to be the exact middle of the piece of land. I stood at the tallest point, envisioning it to be the center of the entire universe.

The gentle wind and the soft grass caressed me as I gazed skyward, anticipating the visual excellence of that midday summer sky.

When my eyes opened, I took a step forward entering, seemingly, into another world. The meadow began to swirl around me. The edges of the forest, there just a moment ago, receded as the small grassland grew in size until it filled my entire vision. The blue sky, once vividly clear, was suddenly filled with light of a different kind. Blue light—a deeper blue than was possible.

The world as I knew it was suspended, and in its place, was one where only I existed. I peered upward into the dazzling blue light as my outstretched arms felt the gentle touch of the waving stalks. I was definitely connected to this place.

Without warning, way up in the top of the sky, five white pinpoints of light appeared. To my astonishment, they formed a perfect pentagon.

Were these stars? They couldn't be, it was the middle of the day.

Then all at once, they darted across the sky! Still arranged in a five-part array with open sky in-between, they had relocated—instantly. With a blink of an eye they were in one spot, then another. And without a sound. Before I could think about how it might have happened, they zoomed again! They disappeared from one spot and appeared much farther across the arc of the sky, again instantly.

Turning to my left for a better view, I blinked long and hard before peeking again. The glowing pentagon light formation was still there, shining before me.

Time stood still during my private show. A magnificent scene of lights danced along the blue yonder filling me with joy and wonder. I laughed aloud as they popped and flicked their way across the sky—*my* sky.

Then, as suddenly as they appeared, they were gone. They zipped so far that they disappeared from view. I stood perfectly still. Baffled at what had occurred, yet hoping for another glimpse, I scoured the vast blue above. After several minutes my eyes hurt from the strain, forcing me to give up the search.

Questions flooded my mind.

What were these lights?

Were they spaceships from another planet?

Did I just see a UFO?

I had seen shows on TV about flying saucers and strange lights in the sky.

Were they lights in my personal sky that were only intended for me to see?

As I mulled it over, it felt as if the five lights were for me to see—and no one else. Someone was trying to show me they were there.

I pondered the meaning of that incident for days.

I returned to the meadow many times in the following months, but the lights never returned. However, what I had seen in the open field, along with friends visiting at night, taught me at a young age that our perception is not merely of the earthly plane. We can discern many events and things outside of the physical if we are attuned to seeing, and hearing them.

What is reality? Does this universe offer everything we can experience? Mainstream science tells us that only the Newtonian world—the one we can see, hear, and touch—is real. But is it true we need only look at things from this perspective? That is hard science, and if it cannot be proven by testing using actual physical instruments then there is no way to prove it. Thus, we are told by some it must not exist.

Science, however, is beginning to understand that beyond the realm of physical matter of time and space are additional dimensions with infinite possibilities, existing independently of the laws of motion. The world quantum physics describes is a very different one full of non-deterministic and infinite possible realities.

I believe that as spiritual beings, Soul, we all have the ability, and the opportunity, to experience these alternative realities and explore the ones quantum physicists predict do exist. Both science and religion now seem to allow for a broader definition where many universes exist, some above the laws of time and space.

In the meadow that day, through my elevated state of awareness, I was able to witness events existing beyond the physical laws of time and space. And it held special meaning. The cabin enclosed by the forest canopy represented the empty shell of physical body—spiritless. The pine forest depicted people sheltering children from the greater realities—the open sky. The well was dry—symbolizing no nourishment for Soul.

What would this look into the worlds beyond prove to me? How would it inspire me to look deeper into my own inner reality? Those answers would have to wait until more experiences took place in my life, which did not take long.

Later that summer my whole world abruptly changed in one pivotal moment. It is during such times that you may or may not realize it, but the future you are moving into holds little comparison to the past.

Mother's Love

We have heard it is good to get out of our comfort zone. Sometimes, being *uncomfortable* is the only way to unfold spiritually. Think about it—if we never experience change, then how will we grow? Growth *demands* that we change, drop the comfy, and adapt to the "new" brought our way.

Fear is the main impediment to change. Therefore, fear can become the main obstacle to our spiritual growth. Sounds pretty straightforward, doesn't it? Well, in my experience, practice of this principle is a whole lot harder than the theory.

I was blessed with warm caring parents. My father was a wonderful man, a doctor with the unique ability to help many people heal—where other physicians had failed. He worked hard helping patients, which allowed my mom to be home every day spending valuable time with us three boys. My mother taught me my first lessons about unconditional love, in this lifetime at least.

Unconditional love is the highest form love can achieve. It's a pure love that just is, without conditions. We simply love, that's it. Love is all there is. I was lucky to have a mom that loved me the way she did.

I do not recall my parents ever fighting, or even arguing. Pretty good situation, right? Nothing is perfect, however.

Dad smoked cigars and lit one up in the evening when he got home from work. Mom was a chain smoker. Often, I saw her light a new cigarette from the dying embers of the latest butt.

All that smoke made me nauseous. We lived in a cold climate, so windows were closed during the long winter months.

Actually, the fact my parents smoked so heavily may have been a blessing. I grew so sick of the smell that it steeled in my mind the habit would *not* happen to me. One day while walking my favorite path into the woods, I observed the clean cool air enter my nose and make its way into the lungs. I gazed around at the magnificent trees while breathing in the energizing air. At that very moment, I made a commitment to *never* smoke!

Mom got sick. It seemed all those years of four packs a day caught up with her. It was breast cancer, but I have a feeling smoking was the true culprit.

She tried everything to treat this modern disease—carrot juice cleanses, fasting, radiation treatments, and surgery. No stone was left unturned. She did her best to keep up appearances, especially for us boys, whom she wanted to protect from the harsh reality of her affliction.

My father, known as "Doc" even to us boys, was one of the finest doctors in our part of the country. He had good success working with difficult diagnoses, so word spread about this wonderful man and his small practice located in, what appeared to be, an overgrown garage. He drew patients from our area as well as neighboring states. He also had the occasional patient fly all the way from Europe to seek his unique style of practice. Once he told me of a man who flew to his tiny office in northwestern Pennsylvania from the Soviet Union. He heard of my father's practice from a friend in the USA and sought him out for the treatment of radiation poisoning.

Many of his patients had visited some of the finest medical institutions in the country, yet could not get well. In many cases, my father's unique style provided answers for desperate people—and they told their friends. Often, they filled up vans with family, friends, and neighbors to make the trek to see Dr. Terrell. As a result, Doc turned away many patients—accepting only the most difficult cases.

My father, however, was not able to help my mother with her illness. I'm sure it frustrated him as much as it did her.

It was a late summer day of my 10th year. Everyone else in the family needed to go out of the house so Doc asked me to keep an eye on mom. I wondered why he asked me to do this. After all, she was a grown-up that should not have needed supervision. She had been sick, that was no secret, but I did not really know just how much she was hiding until I entered her room.

I agreed to keep an eye on mom as I watched dad rush out the front door. The house was quiet and still—everyone was gone. It was time to do my job.

I inched toward her cracked open bedroom door, trying to be quiet so as not to wake her. Gently pushing the door forward, I squeezed through and tiptoed in.

Not much light shone into the wood paneled bedroom. The curtains were drawn shut to make it easier to sleep, but combined with the dark musty carpet, it set a dismal tone. Luckily, the room was free of smoke, with a medicinal odor lingering in its place.

I crept slowly past her dresser toward the corner where a dining chair had been placed. It was never there before. I guess it was added since mom now needed to be checked on.

I sat on the edge of the hard-wooden seat as my eyes adjusted to the lighting, or lack of it. I expected her to be asleep. Stretching my neck to peek onto the huge king bed, I realized she was awake—wide awake.

I did not notice that her usual gorgeous blonde beehive hairdo was disheveled. Nor did I pay attention to her favorite pink nightgown, partially covered in floral sheets, drenched in sweat. What I did see was much worse. I looked on in horror as her entire body convulsed. Her head tossed back and forth in a feverish malaise, but I knew it was not a fever tormenting her. She was in a great deal of pain.

I had never heard such helpless sounds. Each groan ripped my tiny heart open.

I sat—frozen—not knowing what to do. What *could* I do? She was in so much agony she did not even know I was in the room. And if she had known what I was seeing, she would feel even worse—if that was even possible.

Amazingly, I felt her love and protection, even in her severely compromised state.

I could not imagine what she was feeling. I cried; for her, for myself, for my aching heart that connected us. I prayed to God my family would return and hopefully they would be able to help her.

The evening seemed like it would never end. I wondered why my father put me in such a horrible position. She would not have allowed me to see her like that. Although her body looked fairly strong as it always had, the pain told another story. The real one. The story that would never be told by her lips.

I was thankful the pain eased up enough for her to fall asleep.

My tears stopped.

The front door shut and dad rushed into the room. He nodded to me, motioning it was okay to go. As I left the room, I turned back and saw him remove an amber bottle from a white paper bag. Dad was getting mom's pain medication filled at the pharmacy—something only *he* could do.

A few days later, mom was admitted into the hospital. Another couple of weeks passed when our occasional babysitter temporarily moved in to look after my mom's three boys.

I expected her to get better. I mean, when people get sick, eventually they all get better, right?

On a mid-August day, not unlike the one earlier in the summer when I had witnessed the five lights in the sky, I was outside playing in the yard. It was a beautiful day and I did not want to come inside because I was having so much fun.

"Jeff, come inside!" my dad called.

That was odd. *Why was dad home?*

"Ok", I agreed and headed for the house.

My father met me at the back door and instantly I knew something was wrong. First, he was never home from work at that time of day. Second, he did not make a habit of addressing me first when I came in.

My father was a good provider, is what my grandmother always said. He loved his job and worked hard. When he came home, he usually said very little to us kids. Typically arriving around 9:00 pm, we were usually already tucked in bed. Today, however, he was home around 6:00 pm. Very strange.

Before my father could speak the words, I knew what he was going to say.

"Your mother is gone", he mumbled.

My mind, even though it already *knew*, suddenly refused to believe the words I heard.

"What do you mean, dad, mom is gone?", I questioned.

After a slight pause, he swallowed hard and managed to squeak out a few words.

"Your mother has died", he clarified.

My thoughts raced back to the picture burned in my mind of my mother twisted in pain, upon her death bed.

I realized I would never see her again.

The finality of my mother's death was revealed to me, but the recognition of this fact would take a lot longer to sink in. The one person who loved me unconditionally was gone from my life. *What now? What would the future hold? How would I be able to go on?* I was numb; grieving.

Why did I need to go through such pain, loss, and suffering? With nowhere to turn and no one to guide me, I started spending more time alone. I needed comfort—yes, I was in a lot of pain myself—emotionally.

The next several years were bleak. I wandered through days, sad and lonely, feeling sorry for myself. I had retreated from people as I searched for where I belonged. My friends had all but given up on me—I suppose they thought I *wanted* to be left alone. Perhaps they were right, but I really did not know how to deal with the agonizing emotions smothering me.

The years that followed were punishing. I was depressed. I was angry. *Why had God taken away the one person who truly loved me?*

Although I miss my mother and think of her every day, the lessons in love we shared allowed me to experience unconditional love. The void left behind forced me to look in other places to find the love I no longer felt.

Many years later—with the benefit of time—I was blessed to recognize the meaning of that pivotal moment in a spiritual context. It was time for me to move on from my small protected world of a child. I was comfortable—felt safe; and I wanted to stay in my happy place forever. But change was forced upon me. And as I have learned, change leads to spiritual growth.

Little did I know, much more spiritual growth was waiting around the corner—all I had to do was catch the school bus for my next big lesson!

The Gift on the School Bus

There was no comfort in my hollow heart since the day my father called me in from playing to tell me what I already somehow knew. My mother was gone. She had lost her cancer battle. In her absence, I realized all the love she had given to me—always there with whatever I needed. I thought that was the way it would always be.

I was depressed for the following few years. With her gone I was lost myself, struggling to find my way in a cold lifeless world where her love no longer protected me. Fortunately, an ordinary event transpired and propelled me out of a downward cycle filled with loneliness and self-pity. I did not have to travel, seek, or search—because it happened on a typical day while riding home on a school bus.

The empty seat next to mine clearly separated me from the others. Although the bus was filled with kids, I heard nothing. Felt nothing. I was stuck inside a tiny miserable bubble.

Peering through the dirty bus window, I observed that the formerly colorful autumn scene had become a distant memory. The showers days ago had washed the remaining crimson leaves off the trees and swept them into the gutter. Left were lonely branches fending for themselves against the perpetual rain.

Thick steel-gray clouds limited the sun to the role of merely highlighting the ghostly gloom. Sadly, the weather perfectly matched my mood. I sat still, glaring out the window, as the freezing plastic seat stole its way through my thin pants.

I was looking at nothing, but searching for something.

A hazy film of mist framed the monochrome scene outside, creating a dream-like quality. The formerly real world began morphing into an active movie scene. Fuzzy edges connected, yet separated, me from the world outside—I could not tell where my space ended and the movie began.

I drifted away as the landscape movie slowly played. The 3-D picture moved back and forth, forward and back, until it began merging with a picture in my mind. The scene stagnated—allowing it to crystallize into a single image—hypnotizing me. My mental apparatus was suspended for a moment, freeing me to explore an alternative universe.

A vision of a recent problem I had been mulling over

appeared. As I stepped into the "dream", another seemingly unrelated issue materialized before me.

How were these two events related, and why did they appear on the screen of my mind?

I closed my eyes against the plastic image streaming through the bus window. Then something struck me—nothing I could see, but rather an impression I could feel. And I *felt* it come alive.

I sensed a pattern had emerged. Like wavelengths on a monitor the lines moved up, then down, then up. High, then low, then high again. Waves of still photos highlighting moments of my life rushed by. My highs. My lows.

Shocked by the lucid vision, my eyes opened and once again gathered in the colorless landscape drifting past the window. Gently my eyelids met—returning to the vision.

Yes, there was an order superimposed on the events in my life. In its totality, I saw the pattern mirror the challenges I had faced.

I searched my memory banks for other events. Yes, they too seemed to follow this ebb and flow. Reviewing the past few months, then years, I clearly saw a rhythm to my life's experiences. Each and every time I had been given a challenge, I had also graciously been allowed time to work it out before another surfaced. Each situation seemed to present itself at a pace I could handle. Barely, but yes, I managed each one.

How could this be? Don't events just arbitrarily happen?

It seemed these affairs were playing out according to some master plan. There was no way it was random; the pattern was crystal clear and had been happening my entire life. I was puzzled.

If this pattern existed—and it definitely *did*—then something, or someone, of a divine nature must have a hand in it. Something working above this earth world had to be involved.

Was this, in-fact, God's handiwork?

It had to be a higher power, I mused. There was really no other explanation—God must be behind it all. I saw myself just able to handle what God gave me to work out and it felt like grace. The problems were tough, but they seemed lighter now somehow. And I physically *felt* lighter, too.

Frozen in stunned silence, I tried to gather in all I had witnessed.

I had just recognized one of the most profound and liberating principles about my life and I needed a moment to let it sink in. Contradictory, the realization seemed so natural, like I was simply remembering it.

A warmth in my core radiated as I twisted around in the seat. Awakened with life, I observed the energy swirling throughout the bus. The boys in the seat beside me were playing jokes on the two girls in front of them. Behind me, I knew the whispering and giggling was about a certain boy they thought was cute. Everyone was happily chatting and playing. The weather outside did not seem to bother them in the least. Perhaps, the depressing weather outside did not match their moods, so they paid no attention to it.

And at that moment, I too paid no mind to the scene outside the bus. Something had changed, shifted. The warmth within noticeably expanded, generating a new feeling.

A smile crept across my face. For the first time since the loss of my mother, I felt loved. Yes, it was love lifting me ever so slightly above the dreary mood I was stuck in just a few moments earlier. I realized someone else was taking care of me, making sure I had the tools, understanding, and all I needed to survive in this world.

What a gift!

I could not fully grasp all this realization implied back then, but now recognize it as an essential turning point. It enabled me to understand the flow of my life and see God's loving hand in it.

If we can recognize that we are Soul, a divine being,

living—in the moment—in a physical body, then we have a global spiritual perspective. We are Soul. As Soul, we realize we are a part of God. A spark of God. And we exist as Soul because of God's love for us. If we can tune into the love from God, then events in our lives align with what God wants for us. Our purpose. Our mission.

Life becomes smoother once we begin truly living in this state. Also, as I learned on the school bus that day, there is a loving pace and rhythm to life's experiences that we need to allow to work. It is a paradox; the more we surrender to Spirit and the will of God, the more we get what we need. And ironically, the results far exceed any visions my limited mind could conjure up.

It was time to walk a new path leading me out of the gloomy prison I had been inhabiting. I still struggled with bouts of depression and loneliness for many years, all my problems did not magically disappear. But I had been given a wonderful gift that day. It was the realization that God was helping me in my life and had shown me a different type of love. Yes, my mother was gone, but now I recognized a love that had been there the whole time, and one that would not be going away. God had not abandoned me after all, rather God loved me. God had always loved me, and would continue to love me—unconditionally.

That bus ride though bleak landscape had transported me to a new level of consciousness, one allowing me to recognize the greater scope of life, one that extends into the very heart of God. With love in my heart, I was ready to explore more about religion and God.

On Your Own Journey to God

The awakening on the school bus allowed me to see an inner connection, the orchestration of my life's events according to a divine plan. Experiencing myself as Soul—my true identity—I have come to realize there is no separation between me and God, we are all an extension of that energy. We are God's love in expression, inhabiting a physical body on this planet.

When tuned in to God's love, we experience ourselves as that Divine Being. With love in our hearts, we have the power to transform our lives and break free from the bonds of our self-imposed virtual prisons to realize our full potential as Soul, a divine spark of God.

I understand these principles today, but when I was fifteen, a profound insight awaited me as I contemplated an argument I had heard about which church taught truth.

The sun shone brightly that summer Sunday morning as I squeezed into the back passenger seat of my cousin's AMC Gremlin car. A few months earlier, my family had invited me to tag along to a non-denominational Christian church and I agreed to give it a try. I had been making the trip for several months—almost every week—and was looking forward to the experience again that day.

We all enjoyed the loving environment shared by those in attendance every week, and looked forward to the affectionate embraces. It was the first time I had felt the familiar warmth I had searched for since the loss of my mother and was thankful for the friendly congregation uplifting me with so much love.

Now this church was not right around the corner; in fact, it was twenty miles from my home. For a car full of teens, it was quite a distance to travel but, like me, they were looking for love, too.

The others joined me in the car ready for the thirty-minute drive. The mood was always happier on the way back home—especially for me that day because I had come forward at the end of the service to be baptized. I was joyful and happy to have found my new home.

As we drove away, my cousins, brother, and I, were engrossed in lively discussion. They congratulated me on coming forward and receiving the baptism and membership in the church.

Amongst all the joy inside, I had a problem. While sharing loving embraces of celebration as I left the church, I overheard two ladies talking. They were discussing a specific belief another local Christian church held that was clearly wrong as far as they were concerned. They both agreed the teachings of our church spoke the truth and the other had it wrong. The statement put a huge damper on my otherwise joyful mood.

As I sat in the back of the Gremlin mulling it over, the words I heard began to haunt me. I wondered, *how was our church able to capture the perfect truth?*

The drive home seemed to take a little longer than usual but we eventually arrived at my house. A quick "thank you", to my cousin for the ride and I was on my own for the remainder of the day.

First things first, I was starving. It was well past my usual lunch time. I changed into my jeans and t-shirt then quickly ate my sandwich. I flew out the door toward my best friend Dennis's house with nothing on my mind except cars.

Dennis and I had recently become friends again after a few years apart. As I mentioned before, the shock of my mother's death caused me to retreat from my friends. However, a miracle happened and brought us back together. Unbeknownst to one another, we had both purchased classic Chevrolet Bel-Air's, his a 1955 and mine a 1957. Our common love of fixing up our old Chevrolets had brought us back together again and I could not have been happier about it.

Dennis lived only a few doors down and his backyard boasted a structure—similar to an old barn—which was the perfect place for our passionate hobby.

Although only three houses away, the route was punctuated by a series of thick grassy yards mounded up between sunken stony driveways. Running the hilly path was like surfing ocean waves. A roller coaster of sorts. As I took off, the breeze in my face was a welcome respite from the burning sun.

I quickly passed the tan home next to mine with the red brick fireplace on the left side. Pushing off from their driveway, arriving at the next yard—the biggest hill of all—I felt a rush! My speed picked up on the way down.

As I crested the last yard, I was suddenly stopped dead in my tracks. Although ready to jump down onto my friend's driveway—my body was stuck. I stood, as the comment made earlier that day by the ladies at church flashed in the forefront of my mind.

How could our church be right and the church across town be wrong?

This single question unexpectedly popped into my mind. Although I was dreaming about my classic car, the words grabbed me again.

Somehow, I knew there was no way one single church taught perfect truth and all others had it wrong.

What about all the Muslims in the middle-east? What about the Buddhists? The Catholics?

What were the chances that any religion, specifically the teachings of one individual church in a rural Pennsylvania town, held the true answers when every other church and religion on earth didn't?

I just couldn't agree.
Still standing.
On the hill.
In the yard.
The answer suddenly came through.
The questions circling my mind were replaced with this

immutable truth.

Every religion was right!

And every belief was right.

Two rights don't make a wrong.

So, I surmised, everybody had to be correct in *their* beliefs. *I* was right, and so was everyone else. Yes, that just *had* to be.

I knew that my beliefs, my truth, was right for me. Others I knew, also believed with the same certainty that they were right about *their* religious beliefs. There was no way they could be wrong, just the same that there was no way I could be wrong. This profound truth floated down and stuck in my mind like a lawn dart.

With this newfound insight, I felt a sense of empowerment as I envisioned each individual, who were right in their own truth, squarely in the drivers' seat on their own personal spiritual quest.

Why did people waste so much time arguing and fighting over differences in their beliefs? Many a war has been waged here on earth for this very reason. The truth of that principle stood out as something very obvious. The only way it could be was this: everyone was involved in their own personal truth, tailored specifically for them and their station along their individual spiritual journey.

The realization finally let go and allowed my feet to slide off the stone wall, landing me squarely onto the driveway. Content in my realization, I was now ready to spend a glorious day surrounded by our cars.

Dennis asked me to help with his '55 Chevy Bel-Air. He needed me to turn the ignition while he closed the choke on the carburetor. I jumped behind the wheel and twisted the key. The engine sputtered to life—and as I heard the roar of the exhaust I realized something. I was in the driver's seat. Literally. Instantly, I recognized the waking dream confirmation that I was actually sitting in the driver's seat in my life—and on my own spiritual quest. Exactly as the words had landed in my consciousness while standing on the hill.

I did not fully realize it at the time, but I was beginning to walk a new path that would result in my break from the Christian church to take another step upon my individual spiritual journey. The adventure of my lifetime awaited me as I was put in charge of my own destiny. I would miss the love I felt from the congregation, but I had a feeling my individual sojourn into personal truth would lift me higher towards the ultimate goal; divine love.

With the relative speed of a lawn dart hitting the ground, my realizations became rungs on a ladder enabling me to climb along on my own spiritual journey. The self-discovery that awaited led directly to knowledge gained previously—before this current lifetime. Yes, it was time to gain a much deeper understanding of Soul—and that meant exploring a previous lifetime.

8

LESSON FROM A PAST LIFE

On a Sailboat with a Fear of Water

Reincarnation, defined as the rebirth of Soul in a new body, is a core principle in many religions. Although most people do not recall past lives, it is believed Soul lives through a plethora of lifetimes interacting with others, learning lessons, and hopefully resolving karma along the way.

Karma is defined in the dictionary as the sum of a person's actions in this and previous states of existence, viewed as deciding their fate in future existences. It is cause and effect. There are times an experience in our past effects the present.

Have you ever been confused by a repetitive cycle in your life that makes no sense based on knowledge from this lifetime? Does a baffling event or scenario continuously surface? We can request, or ask on the inner, to receive guidance about perplexing situations such as these.

If fortunate, we are offered a peak into the past—*our* past.

It is a magical gift when deeply intertwined meaning, to seemingly unrelated situations, is revealed. Once the mysteries are uncovered, connecting ties might be recognized. Spiritual tools—including the HU song and contemplative exercises—can help bring clarity, insight, and understanding which could result in our burdens or challenges resolving. That is, if it is in alignment and in the best interest of all involved for the karma to be rectified.

I was blessed to experience one of those profound moments several years back when I took up sailing. Although I loved the wind in my face while gliding across the waves, a silent internal struggle ensued as I battled increasingly irrational fear while out on my sailboat. Something had to give. I sought out answers, never expecting a vivid, cold experience from a past life to reveal itself.

Before I took up cycling, sailing was my favorite hobby. I was first introduced to it in 1983, while living in Charlottesville, Virginia, by a friend of mine, Paul, who owned a ski and surf shop. Conveniently, he also gave lessons on those sports.

I will never forget the first day he invited me out to sail windsurfers at a small lake near town. I was intrigued since I had seen people sailing the boards on TV while visiting Hawaii. It looked more like flying, I mean they barely touched the water periodically while mostly riding the wind. It looked like a lot of fun so I readily agreed to give it a try, certain I would not be flying over wave tops with my hair on fire.

We rode together to the lake where Paul launched the board into the calm water. The wind was almost imperceptible.

Not too tough of conditions for a first time.

"You first", he said.

I looked his way quizzically, then back at the sailboard gently bobbing on the shoreline.

What the heck, it's not going to kill me.

"OK", I said, then stepped onto the board. He rambled off a quick tutorial before sending me on my way. *What was I thinking?* I did not know the first thing about sailing yet there I was.

Paul barked commands from his position on shore about how to position the board, the sail, and my feet.

Although I ended up spending more time *in* the water than *on* it that first day, it was a lot of fun and a profound experience.

The sensation of being on the water with merely the wind moving me along was intoxicating. No roaring motors, but rather the melodic sound of waves lapping against the board created an invisible connection to the environment. A primal feeling it was—man, the wind, and the water—all working together to create an awesome, liberating, and unforgettable experience.

In hindsight, it is interesting that my first sailing endeavor was on a sailboard since it is one of the most difficult crafts to master. The board and sail each point in different directions while the body weight is balanced perfectly against the sail and mast—oh, and with the push of the wind changing constantly. No small feat. It was my first and last time on a sailboard but one thing was certain—I was hooked on sailing!

After nearly ten years of adventures on borrowed and rented craft, I purchased two sailboats, a Capri 14.2 and a Sunfish. They were moored along the shoreline of a 1,700-acre lake conveniently located at the end of my street. This enabled me to sail—a lot. After work, I would grab the sail bag, jog down to the lake, rig up my vessel, and shove off onto the peaceful water. I was definitely improving as a sailor, and in-fact, managed to spend most of my time *out* of the water.

But secretly I had a problem; kind of a big one. As good as I was, something was holding me back. I figured all the time I had spent on the lake would have gotten me used to being on the water—but not the case. In fact, I was fearful of something and it was steadily getting worse.

I could no longer deny it, I had to face the truth of the matter—I was deathly afraid of the water.

I finally put my finger on it and faced the reality of my predicament—I loved sailing and being on the water, but I was unnaturally afraid of the water itself. I mean, having a healthy respect for it is useful when you are a sailor, but the fear I felt was *not* natural. The realization that I needed to do something about the fear—or else find a new hobby—weighed heavily on my mind.

One day, I bravely decided to explore the meaning behind the fear by utilizing my spiritual toolbox. I quieted myself and got into a comfortable position to do a contemplative exercise. I visualized my sailboat, the water, and the intense feelings. After a few deep breaths, I sang HU to help align myself with the Holy Spirit.

Instantly, my inner vision revealed a glimpse of myself—yet I was someone else. Recognizing the scene from another time entirely, I knew it was a past life.

Scruffy men in tattered sun-bleached clothing surrounded me on a sailboat. Looking through the eyes of my past, I knew we worked together in the open sea, day in and day out. I deeply respected, even feared, some of them.

I took in the entire scene, noticing we were sailing in a churning sea at a pretty good clip. Why? Because we were whalers.

American settlers started the whaling industry in the mid 1600's. The native Americans hunted smaller crustaceans mainly and only took whales that drifted up on shore. There is no evidence they were hunted systematically. In the following decades, men rowed out to sea in small boats hunting the whales just off the coast. By the mid 1700's, the nearby seas had been fished out, so the whalers took to using single-masted sloops and even two-masted brigs to travel further out in search of these leviathans of the deep. At that time, whale oil was the only commercial source of oil for energy use, drilling in the ground had not yet been discovered.

Whales are the largest animals in the history of the earth. Even the largest dinosaur that ever walked on land is no match for the great whale in size.

Whaling was one of the most dangerous jobs

imaginable. Many ships went out but never returned, and almost every voyage that did was touched with tragedy.

I stood, in the single-masted sloop, wondering why I was out at sea doing such a dangerous job.

But somehow, I knew.

I was on that ship because I thought being a whaler would fix me somehow. I was a young man and the adventure, danger, and reward of killing the great beast of the sea was appealing. It fueled my ego. I was a whaler, hunting the largest animal in the history of the earth. I thought somehow that would make me a man, someone to be respected, and even feared by the younger men of our village. That was to be my mission, my quest fulfilled.

The life was grueling and extremely lonely, but I felt a sense of purpose in the work. I loved the sea and was energized by the raw experience of life on the edge, working hard with no regard for my body. Yes, my ego drove me to take enormous risks. The men I worked with were the rough ones, though, and some thought them mad. But that was part of the allure—*that* was exactly the man I *wanted* to be.

Many men met their death in such profession. It was the tremendous seduction of profit that drove many of us to risk everything. For me, I was trying to find myself.

The wind had picked up and the roiling sea was rising ever higher as it began to break against our bow. A storm had suddenly descended upon us.

The men on board were experienced sailors but also very superstitious. The sea was a living thing filled with spirits, just like the enormous animals we chased around in it. The sea, and the spirits moving upon its face, spoke and warned them we were in trouble. Everyone cowered in fear.

My mates and I were headed into the "belly of the beast".

I looked to the older men for answers, hoping to learn from their experience. The water was angry. An ominous energy consumed us and turned our faces a similar green color as the boiling sea. We tried to sing songs to lift our spirits but could not shake the feeling of doom.

A massive gust of wind tore through the rigging, shredding our meager sails. The sky and the sea merged into one monstrous torrent shattering and tossing our little boat of match sticks into the air, then smashing it upon the pounding waves.

The immense power ravaged our craft. Never had I felt so small against my world. I thought myself a brave and proud man but in that moment, was more like a small child being schooled by an angry father. As our little boat tore apart, we each tried to save ourselves. Men clung to shards of the vessel in the foam surrounded by a most horrific wind.

Alas, the mast I clung to plunged into the frigid churning sea, shoving me deep into the mouth of the beast.

In that instant, underneath the water, I was terrified of death.

What would become of me? Why was this happening just as I "found myself"?

What purpose did my life serve?

I was alone in life, and would be alone in death—dashed by the very thing I loved, the sea. An angry God had demolished our boat and my dream right before me. I was angry and felt abandoned by God in those last moments of life.

A decision had to be made.

Should I give in to the raging sea and let it take me?

Or should I keep fighting?

Ultimately, the decision was made for me as the last breath left my defeated body.

The helpless corpse became one with the sea.

My eyes slowly opened.

The HU song I sang along with on the CD player had ended without my notice. I came out of contemplation outwardly shaken as my mind reeled from what I had witnessed, reflecting on my life as a whaler.

However, in reliving the scene an epiphany helped me realize the truth.

God had *not* abandoned me.

I had abandoned God.

God had given me the wonderful gift of freedom, but I was not ready to see it. I was free to live the life I wanted but was too consumed in the glory of the hunt and what it would say to others about this brave proud man who tamed the mystical beasts of the sea. Soberingly, my ego had gotten the best of me. My need for status, due to lack of self-esteem, caused me to place myself in a dangerous line of work that ultimately cost me everything.

And this, lifetimes later, was the reason for my present fear of water. I experienced a death of the physical body by drowning in a most horrible circumstance. It certainly made sense.

Miraculously, my perplexing fear of water gradually eased over the following months allowing me to become more comfortable on my sailboat. I was finally free. No longer did fear hold me back from enjoying my hobby or improving as a sailor.

I was blessed with another priceless gift. God had used a fear of water to encourage me to review a past life—one that held important lessons for me in my personal spiritual unfoldment here and now.

I relived an experience and learned something from it I had failed to see at the time. Although obvious in hindsight, it was a mistake to choose my profession to make others respect or fear me. The ego drove me to risk, and lose, my life. It also blinded me to the greatest gift of all—God's love.

I had abandoned God during those lonely years but now have a chance to embrace God's love. There is always another chance, another opportunity, to get it right spiritually. Often experiences present themselves repeatedly, urging us to learn and unfold to our true spiritual nature, that of being one with the Holy Spirit—and one with

God. In our own time. In our own unique way.

Learning from past lives is a golden opportunity for growth. It is but one instrument inside our spiritual toolbox at our disposal anytime day or night. Dreams are yet another option available to us. We have the ability to gather information from multiple planes, or dimensions, for our use here and now—in the current physical state. And with dream journaling and a little patience, one of my dreams helped solve a work conundrum I had faced for months.

9

KNOWLEDGE FROM A DREAM

The Invention

Dreams are a hot discussion topic now-a-days, but what actually are they? Are they bits and pieces from daily occurrences scrambled and re-hashed for our nightly entertainment? Are they simply leftover mind clutter as some proclaim? I say no—dreams are much more than what conventional wisdom says. Based on personal study and observation, I believe they are actual events; as real as the ones that take place while we are awake.

Imagine a dreamer—then switch places with them for a moment. Now, who are you? I assert that the dreamer is us—who we *truly* are—Soul, a perpetual divine being living in a constant state of "now". Soul experiences no birth, death, sleep, or waking. Soul—you and I—are the eternal dreamer, living a constant "dream" be it in this world or in any of the other realms.

Since Soul does not sleep when the physical body does, it has the unique opportunity to encounter the higher worlds without interference from this physical plane. If we can tune into those nocturnal adventures a fuller life awaits, a more complete existence. Talk about multi-tasking!

Sleep is just another way to gain experience while living in a human body. Since adopting this attitude I look forward to a little shut-eye because I know I am getting more out of those "unconscious" hours.

What we call "dreams", I believe, is the portion of events happening in alternate realities that can be translated into something our physical brain and senses can recognize. Much of what goes on "out there" responds to the laws of physics governing the "matter" that exists at the vibratory level of that specific plane of existence. Here on Earth, where perhaps a lower vibration and a different set of physical laws pervade, we simply cannot bring most of the details back because they do not make sense here. The experiences must be filtered—scrambled by our mind, leaving only a tiny remnant of the actual occurrence so our physical brains can understand and interpret it for our own benefit in the physical world.

How many times have you awoken from a dream with a vivid understanding, only to have it fade fast once you are fully awake? For me, it is that in-between time when my body is still half asleep, when I try to jot something down on paper. It is tough, because once writing begins I become more connected to this physical plane, creating more distance from the dream state. Give it a try, though. No matter how insignificant the remembrance seems to your waking senses, it could be a puzzle piece for you.

There is much literature available concerning dream study and interpretation. While there may be some good information gleaned from these writings, we are each the best interpreters of our own dreams. Much of the texts revolve around symbols. While I recognize the importance of them in dream interpretation for myself, I do not believe in universal symbols. Instead, we each draw from our own bank of experiences and thus, the symbols that appear are meaningful to us, and us alone.

I personally work with an inner guide, who helps maximize the effectiveness of my inner life. Upon awakening, I am nudged to explore clues from dream memories available to assist me with decisions, emotional troubles, and possibly karmic situations I was not aware of.

Not only can dreams help us spiritually, often they can be a source of guidance in the physical world for some very earthly uses. So, dreams are for our benefit spiritually *and* practically.

It was in a dream that Friedrich August Kekulé discovered the exact arrangement of the carbon atoms in what became known as the Benzene Ring. Kekulé had been working hard to solve how the Benzene molecule could be arranged. He knew it somehow had to contain six hydrogen atoms and six carbon atoms.

The laws of chemistry known in 1872, did not allow for such an arrangement to be formulated. Kekulé, tired from working on this chemical riddle, dozed off. In a dream, he saw the image of two snakes twining together in a mass of flames. Suddenly, the two serpents grabbed each other's tails in their mouths to form a ring. Like the charms on a bracelet, the carbon and hydrogen atoms lined up perfectly to form the Benzene molecule.

When he awoke, he knew what he saw in the dream state was the answer to the riddle. He quickly sketched up the image. He and his colleagues confirmed through experimentation that the model was perfectly correct. They had to rewrite some of the laws of chemistry, but sure enough, the dream had revealed the correct arrangement of the Benzene molecule.

His mind—normally a very *useful* tool—had held him back. The conventional wisdom of the day dictated the Benzene molecule must conform to the laws that had thus-far been established. It was only by going to the higher worlds in the dream, where none of the restrictions existed, that Kekulé could transcend his mind *and* the minds of others working on the problem, to advance the science.

I can personally attest to this phenomenon because I, too, have discovered answers to difficult problems in the dream state. As a Sales Engineer, I work with clients on solutions to make their machines work more efficiently.

Most of the problem solving happens during the daylight, but one situation needed my mind to step aside for the answer to come—and that only happens at night.

A large customer with hundreds of machines in facilities all over the United States had been dealing with a difficult problem for many years. They used air suction going through a control valve to sort their products. This valve turned a vacuum on and off at a high rate of speed. All the activity created an insidious dust cloud that got sucked into the machine by the vacuum, quickly causing a clog. They were spending a huge amount of money replacing this expensive valve because it was not easily cleaned or repaired. The debris also rubbed against the internal components which quickly wore out the parts—every four months to be exact.

This component was the industry standard used on virtually every machine the world over in similar applications. I think that was why no one thought to use a different device. Instead, they lived with the expense and trouble associated with constantly replacing it.

Somehow, deep inside I knew there had to be a better way to accomplish the task—a device to replace the failing component that would work without falling victim to the detrimental dust cloud. I cannot say how I knew, it just seemed there *had* to be a better way.

I worked on the problem for months, failing to improve upon the industry standard being used. Still, a nagging feeling of "knowing there was something better" continued to haunt my efforts.

Frustrated, I eventually stopped beating my head against the wall and instead decided to let the problem go. I figured I must be wrong and resigned myself to the reality there probably was not a better solution. After-all, if the finest minds in the industry thought this was the only way, they were probably right.

A few nights later I woke up around midnight with a crystal-clear dream image in my mind.

Could it really be that easy? No way!

Really, could a mechanism this simple in construction really work?

Perhaps it could, I mused. Moreover, the way it was designed, it would not get dirty—even in the presence of all that dust! In fact, this type of design would use the vacuum to sweep itself clean.

I fumbled around the dimly lit bedside table for my dream notebook to quickly sketch out the vision. After completing the crude drawing, I sat for a moment on the edge of the bed studying my rough design. Yes, this idea may work, but I was sure there had to be something to prevent it from performing all the complex tasks it needed to do. I gently slid the notebook back onto the night stand, crawled under the covers, and returned to dreamland.

By morning I had forgotten about the vision and went about my routine.

Later in the evening, I noticed the "napkin sketch" on the nightstand. In my home office, I carefully redrew the mechanism. This time, however, the image came through with significantly more detail.

As butterflies fluttered in my stomach, I knew this simple device could work.

The valve only had one moving part and would be self-cleaning. Yes, amazingly, it would vacuum itself clean as it worked! Also, the moving parts could be designed to fit closely—yet not rub against each other as they did in the current one. Not only was it simple, but it would not wear out. Yes, indeed, I was onto something.

During bicycle rides in the evenings, I simply rolled the image of the device lightly in my mind and allowed the universe to work on it. I realized a working model was necessary to get others interested in pursuing my invention and on one ride I worked out the exact materials and components needed to construct it.

Finally, after going over the design thoroughly in my

mind, and bringing it into a more practical configuration I could build with physical parts, I worked up the courage to present it to the lead Engineer at the company that manufactured the sorting machines, a PhD in Mechanical Engineering. To my utter astonishment, he seemed to see what I had in mind and asked me to build a prototype he could test. Since I had already worked out the components needed, I was able to quickly build two prototype valves for him to test.

The initial testing went so well that the lead Engineer got behind the project and helped me further refine the design so it could be manufactured economically. The result was even more effective than I would have ever imagined. The new design substantially out-performed the existing technology in what it needed to do and could be operated at twice the speed of the old valve. This allowed them to use half the number of machines they were planning to deploy, saving lots of money for their customer. Furthermore, the design was so simple, it would cost less than the standard valve. Eventually, life testing confirmed this new design would last more than ten years, not four months. None of these outcomes I could have imagined would be possible at the time I sat on the edge of my bed and made my crude sketch at 2:00 am.

This convinced me that I was not actually the inventor. For if I *was*, I would have come up with it utilizing the mental processes I employed early on in my quest—by using my brain. But instead, it was only when I mentally gave up on the design and turned it over to Spirit that the answer came in the dream. I put in the energy, let it go, then allowed the Holy Spirit to take me to the inner planes where the answer was waiting.

I have learned to trust in Spirit to bring things into my life I could not access with merely my mind and the current state-of-the-art. Through the dream state, I could manifest an invention and bring it into the physical realm. The invention exceeded what my physical reality would have allowed me to develop. My mind simply would not have allowed this type of invention to exist, just like the laws at the time Kekulé came up with the arrangement of the Benzene molecule.

This demonstrated that the dream world is much more than what we have been told. It is a place of real things and actual experiences. Some of which, like this invention, can be brought back for our own betterment—and also, for the betterment of others.

So, what we get on the inner is for us to personally decipher. Our thoughts are powerful and able to manifest tangible outcomes. Since the universe hears our positive and negative thoughts—beware of what you ask for. Yet do not be afraid to ask for something you really want, as I did in the next story.

10

POWER OF THOUGHTS

Thoughts Become Things

*P*rentice Mulford, in his famous book, *Thoughts are Things*, talks about the two minds of man. One is the lower mind—of the physical body. The other is the higher mind—of Spirit. He says the lower one is severely limited and resists change at any cost. It believes only "what it is" or "what it has been" is possible. The higher mind, however, is not limited by this construct. It is in touch with the divine and realizes anything is possible—if only we believe.

This concept of the unlimited higher mind revealed itself to me one day in a very unexpected way as I was jogging along a lonely country road.

It was early fall in 1995. Summer had faded fast that year, replaced by cool and crisp autumn days. It had been cloudy and blustery in the morning but the afternoon held promise of sunshine and warmer temperatures, perhaps even into the 70's. I was away from home visiting friends, cooped up inside for a few days. I was anxious to get outdoors for some much-needed exercise, fresh air, and I hoped, sunshine.

I continued checking the weather forecast throughout the day, never letting go of hope. After dinner, I peered out the living room window as the clouds scattered—which was exactly the opportunity I had waited for. The time was right! There would be a tight window, but the temperature should hold for the next hour or two.

My friend had outlined a running course along some back roads near his home, assuring me they were rarely traveled. With the loop marked on the map, I would get in about a 6-mile run, which was perfect. I quickly put on my running shorts, pulled on my t-shirt, laced up my old but sturdy running shoes, and stepped outside. The fresh, cool wind slapped me in the face. In any other situation, my apparel would need an additional layer, but there was no time—my body heat would need to make up the difference.

Now, this was back in the day before the MP3 player was invented and long before iPhones streamed our favorite tunes. If you listened to music on a run you needed a cassette tape player; which I had. After jamming the only tape I had brought with me into the player and clipping it to the waistband of my shorts, I took off at a moderate pace.

Attempting to ignore the chilly air, I shuffled across the green leaf-covered lawn anticipating the run. Technically, maybe it was in the 70's, but it felt much cooler. The golden sun was shining on me as I convinced myself it would be okay.

Leaves were beginning to change color. The spectacular scenery rolling past me grabbed my attention and I soon forgot about the temperature. The sunlight streamed through the fleeing clouds illuminating the entire scene. It was invigorating. I floated along barely feeling the click and crunch of my footfalls on the gravel road. The sun-drenched landscape combined with the energizing breeze gently lifted me up to another place. Excitement within let me know it was going to be a great run!

Normally when running along a roadside with cars passing by I did not listen to music. In this case, however, I felt safe because the roads were in-fact deserted. My friend was right—no cars in sight. The only downside was the music I was listening to. I had only brought one cassette tape with me on the trip—a mistake, I mused—and was quite bored with it.

Wow, I could really go for a little Aerosmith right now, I thought to myself.

The band was one of my favorites and their energetic songs would have made the experience absolutely perfect. I continued running along focusing on the beautiful scenery and the lightness within.

I had sailed along the countryside less than five minutes when I spotted a small black object at the edge of the road. It was just off the gravel surface, clinging to the dirt at the top of a deep ditch. My eyes were glued to the mysterious item causing me to slow my pace to get a better look. Moving ever closer, I noticed that, strangely, it looked like a cassette tape.

Ironically, I was just thinking of tapes moments before. Stunned, I stopped and stooped down to pick up what was most assuredly a cassette tape!

I instantly knew it was homemade.

Beautifully scripted in pencil, it read, "Aerosmith's Greatest Hits".

"What? This can't be!", I enthusiastically exclaimed aloud.

I turned the tape over—then again in my hands, as if somehow the apparition would disappear. I was stupefied. I read, and re-read, the title in disbelief. Finally, I had to admit—yes, clearly written on both sides of the tape was the title "Aerosmith's Greatest Hits".

My brain was not accepting what I was seeing. I looked around instinctively to see who was playing this joke on me. I mean, it had to be a gag, right? There was no way this tape just materialized out of nowhere just because I thought about it.

But I knew no one was around. Even if they were, there was no way they could have known about Aerosmith because I just *thought* about it, I did not say a word aloud.

My body froze, not due to the falling temperature. Perplexed, moments stood still as I tried to figure out what could have happened. First, I envisioned the tape falling out of the sky the moment I thought about it. Ok, not likely. Next, I imagined a more probable scene. Perhaps a couple had been driving down the road when the passenger, sick of hearing the tape, had grabbed it out of the player and tossed it out the window to the dismay of the driver. Sure, *that* was possible.

My brain chimed in with details unexplained. For one, it landed on the shoulder and not *on* the road where it ran the risk of getting smashed by a car tire. Second, the tape was in pristine condition even though it had just rained yesterday. If it had been out in the elements very long it would have gotten dirty inside and out from the raindrops splashing in mud from the shoulder of the road. Third, it was not just an Aerosmith album, but a collection of their greatest songs—*exactly* what I had wished for.

Tape in hand, I surveyed my surroundings again confirming no one else was around.

Finally, I came to terms with the fact that the tape was, indeed, a gift—and I had to accept the gift. So that is what I did. I expressed a silent thank you to God and decided to enjoy the music. Why not?

There was a nervous vibration in my hands as I flipped the cover to the player open, hit the eject button, and extracted the old cassette. I slid it into my waist band then popped in the "Aerosmith's Greatest Hits" tape. It was somewhere in the middle so I spent a few seconds rewinding it to the beginning. I wanted to hear every song.

When it finished rewinding, I hit the play button, expectantly awaiting what I might hear. Within a few seconds, music filled my earphones.

"Dream On" was the title of the first song!

Now I was even more excited because it was my favorite tune by the band. Actually, it was one of my all-time favorite songs, period.

How fitting, I thought to myself. What a perfect symbol

to encapsulate the experience.

And the gifts just kept coming. The meaning of that song was coming through loud and clear. "Dream until your dreams come true" were the lyrics traveling through the headset. I had just, in-fact, dreamed about listening to Aerosmith and because I put it "out there", I was doing just that. I had dreamed about the music and my dream had come true.

So, the real meaning of the experience was becoming clear. Yes, the tape was a wonderful gift from spirit, but I had an even more valuable one. I recognized the love of God coming through the music reassuring me that I was being taken care of. God thought enough of me to send me this precious gift so I would feel loved—*know* that I was loved.

The experience had been so out-of-the-ordinary that I had no choice but to wake up and notice it was happening. If the tape had not just materialized for me in the middle of nowhere I may have missed it. In my experience, important events in our lives often take on a dream-like quality—one that lifts us up and out of our mundane state of mind into a higher level of awareness where the real message can be conveyed.

Certainly, there could be no rational explanation for what had happened. The skeptics would counter it was simply a coincidence, but I do not believe so.

Still stunned, but also thrilled and full of love from the message I had received about the astounding experience, I took off running again. I was connected to the nature surrounding me—trees, birds, wind, falling leaves—as I floated three feet above the pavement. The sun was setting to my left. The yellow-orange light shined brightly, turning the autumn leaves into gold—illuminating the way.

For the rest of my run along the golden path, I grooved to Aerosmith. The love of the Sound and Light of the Holy Spirit moved me forward along my route allowing me a first-hand experience of a grateful heart.

So, thoughts become things. The words of Prentice Mulford were ringing in my ears to the tune of the inspirational music. The higher mind—the spiritual consciousness of man—had intervened that day. It had manifested an event in my life that completely transcended the lower mind.

I was immersed in gratitude. Grasping this concept, I know sometimes we cannot imagine big enough. And the reality of this appeared a few years later when an event changed my life—forever—revealing a future I never could have imagined.

All experiences up to this point were preparing me for my true path. My purpose. My mission of being love and expressing it in service. The path of love lay before me, waiting patiently to reveal a staggering vision.

Part IV: A Mission Together

Jeff & Pam Terrell

11

A SPIRITUAL LOVE STORY

Pam Feels the Energy

*S*tanding in line at the luggage check kiosk wrapped tightly in a soft velvety cape, I sipped black coffee while gazing around the enormous convention center. I saw no warning of the dramatic shift coming within the hour. No flags waved to signal the end of life as I knew it and no sign stood to welcome a new beginning. Unknowingly, a tornado was ready to rearrange my world and all I had to do was be nice and allow a gentleman to advance in front of me in line.

I took a drink while patiently waiting. I noticed a gentleman behind me holding a coat. A quick thought came to mind that it would take me longer to check my bag so I should allow him to go in front of me. I turned to the man and said hello. I politely offered for him to go ahead of me since he only had a coat to check and no luggage. He graciously accepted and moved around me. We introduced ourselves and made light conversation.

Jeff, I repeated his name mentally in an effort to remember it. He stood at the head of the line with his long wool black coat on the counter ready for the next attendant. Leaning against the temporary structure and facing me, he apologized for it taking so long. I heard a voice from the line on my left calling to Jeff. *Wow, that was interesting.* One of the two ladies I met at the seminar, Judy, was there in line next to us *and* she knew Jeff!

He hung around and talked to me until we completed our transactions. Continuing our discussion would have been enjoyable—but visiting the ladies room before entering the auditorium was *mandatory*. We parted ways and I was left with a puzzled sense of disappointment.

Our conversation wasn't over—yet I watched him walk away.

Moments later, still slightly perplexed about my encounter with Jeff, I breezed through security to enter the auditorium.

A nice part of traveling alone is that it allows the opportunity to follow inner guidance and nudges. I had no plan. I did not know where I would sit or who with, and it really did not matter. I was comfortable knowing I would end up exactly where I was supposed to be.

I meandered along the back of the huge room. I liked to sit closer to the stage so took a quick right and made my way up an aisle. I saw one of my friends, and literally skipped along the rows of chairs eager to embrace her. After a brief hug-fest, I continued moving closer to the stage.

Up a few rows to my right, I saw my friend, Judy, waving for me to join her. Luckily, she was positioned *exactly* where I prefer to sit, so happily made my way down her aisle. As I moved nearer, I recognized Jeff, the nice man I let in front of me in the coat line. They had their seats and she motioned for me to take the empty one beside Jeff.

Before my body landed in the seat I was pummeled with pulsing vibes.

Electrical.

Magnetic.

A hundred batteries with jumper cables connected me and Jeff and the amps were dialed up a zillion notches!

I looked into his eyes. Immediately glued, the pull would not allow me to look away. I was lured deep inside to another world; consciousness. A glowing tunnel encased my body and straight ahead a golden opening invited me to step through. A spiritual escalator effortlessly moved me through the ornate arched opening to display magical colors I had never seen.

I was instantly awakened and shuddered as I moved from a life of illness being lived in black and white, to one, instead, filled with healthy vibrant living colors.

Was this how Dorothy in "The Wizard of Oz" felt? I wondered.

Focus, Pam, focus. What was going on? I looked down at the ground to make sure my physical body was not levitating. Confirming I was still physically "on the ground", it took all my might to stay connected enough to communicate.

As I focused on not floating away, Judy told Jeff he should write down his contact information for her—and for me. He wrote on the paper, folded it neatly, and returned it to her. Turning back to me, he slid his cell phone out of his front pocket and entered my Facebook ID and email. I must have given him the right email because he quickly sent a message so I would have his info, too.

Jeff and I were consumed in conversation. Each topic brought up was another thing we had in common. *Did the door experience a few minutes before give him mind reading power? Was there a mind meld like in Star Trek?* I was talking to myself—only better! It was amazing, and addictive. The exchange was energizing, yet so comfortable I could have talked to him forever. I had known him much longer than what seemed on the physical realm.

The program began with a twenty-minute HU song. They were always uplifting and I looked forward to sharing the experience with friends from all around the globe. In an attempt to focus, I shifted to get comfortable in my chair, closed my eyes, and began to sing HU. I heard Jeff singing in my right ear and was cocooned by a loving, slightly overwhelming, energy.

Our HU's were connected and enveloping us. I felt it.

And although my eyes were closed, I saw it appear on my previously blank inner screen. He was a golden "H" and I was the "U", leading millions of shimmering stars as they lovingly swirled around our physical bodies.

We were connected—deeply. The vibration and exquisite color had exploded all the senses in my physical body. We had transgressed time and space. Whatever was going on was much larger and more wonderful than anything I could have imagined for myself—and my life!

By the time the HU song ended, my mind was blown away—and the main program had just started. I gazed around at all the beautiful Souls. Mesmerizing. I was in a state of grace viewing a wave of love that filled the enormous room.

Although filled with gratitude and love beyond measure, I was saddened the event was almost over. So many contradictory emotions pulsed through me as all eyes were transfixed on the jumbo television screens where a short video was shown to end the program.

Tears rolled. I wanted to be held. I wanted to be held and release the tears. I wanted Jeff to notice I was crying and to hold me. Instead, a nice lady on my left put her loving arms tightly around me. I appreciated her kindness and was grateful for the affection.

I pulled myself together, not sure of what to do next. I said goodbye to Judy and the nice lady whom so graciously shared a hug. Jeff got up to leave, he seemed emotional also. I asked him what he was doing next and he said he was driving to the airport. Of course, since he had a rental car. With the shake of a hand, we said goodbye.

I watched him walk away. Again.

The seminar was officially over; I sat and let that sink in a moment as I reluctantly pondered my next move. There were buses shuttling people to the temple and then to the airport. Or if I went to the airport early I could relax and spend some time writing. Yes, that felt right. *So, how was I going to get there?* I got up and exited the auditorium. I moved slowly while observing the uplifting energy that had filled the room over the weekend. I wanted to bottle it to take home!

I arrived at the main entrance of the conference center pondering how to get to the airport. Jeff popped into my mind. He had a car—*and* he was driving to the airport as soon as he checked-out of his hotel. Time was of the essence so I quickly used my phone to reply to the email he sent, asking him if I could catch a ride.

Knowing I had done all I could do with the scenario, I chose to let it go. I had no attachment to the outcome of how I would get to the airport. My divine guidance was very strong so I knew I would be interacting with whoever I was supposed to spend time with.

Even though I let the situation go, I still needed to watch for signs in case an answer jumped out.

Directly in front of me, Judy was volunteering at a table. I recalled her asking for Jeff's contact information. Luckily, he had written his phone number and she willingly shared it with me. Without a second thought, I dialed Jeff's number knowing every moment that went by decreased my chances of hitching a ride.

I nodded and smiled a huge thank you to Judy as I walked away hearing ringing in my left ear.

"Hello", I heard after two rings.

Jeff was sitting in a Starbucks on the lower level of his hotel and had not started his journey. I wasted no time asking for a ride and offering to buy lunch to show my appreciation. He readily agreed to pick me.

I was grateful I could relax before flight time. I was grateful Judy asked for his contact information because he never received my email message. I was also grateful to continue living in the colorful blissful daze I had moved into.

Nothing seemed odd. He had a car, was going to the airport, and I needed a ride. It was a perfect scenario. I patiently waited by the front doors of the convention center.

I had a sense of knowingness that I was going to meet someone during my trip but had no idea who it would be or where they would be from. I was grateful for such a wonderful new friend with so many things in common.

I was not sure what he experienced during the morning session, but I sensed it was equally powerful. Maybe someday I would find words to describe mine and share it with him.

I had travelled a long painful road, lived many lifetimes, and learned a plethora of lessons in preparation for this meeting. I had no sense of our mission together; not yet. Little did I know, a tornado was twisting and intertwining our future—preparing for a magical life of loving service.

Jeff Receives a Vision

Much of what happens in this life takes place on the inner planes first—a reflection of what we experience as Soul. I have heard it said that our life on the physical plane is the dream and when we sleep, daydream, and imagine, we are *truly* awake. I believe in those moments, we are closer to our true state, our true home, as Soul in the worlds of God.

During dreams or periods of contemplation, we allow ourselves to experience the deeper reality, our life as Soul in any of the higher worlds which man calls heaven. The great thing about this is that we do not need to wait until the time of death of the physical body to travel into heaven, we all have the ability to experience heaven here, and now, at any time we wish. This is the great secret.

Standing in front of the coat check station in the Minneapolis Convention Center, I was not aware of the life-changing dream that stood before me. In retrospect, it was probably for the best. Knowing the future can be upsetting, especially if the changes coming profoundly impact the entire course of your life. Besides, knowing what lies ahead, without having the benefit of the experiences leading up to it, could be scary and prevent us from taking the steps needed to realize the coming change—one that was ultimately in our best interest.

I was surprised the woman in front of me in line had insisted I go ahead of her because I only had a coat and she had a bag. Also, she was juggling a cup of coffee in one hand while holding onto the handle of her bag with the other. *What was I thinking in accepting?* If the roles had been reversed, I would have offered her *my* place in line. After all, she had a bag and I only had a coat.

We struck up conversation in the lull that ensued after changing places in line. The coat check attendants who were there just moments earlier had vanished, giving us an opportunity to chat. I learned her name, Pam, and that this was her first attendance at the seminar in quite a few years. I shared it was also my first appearance at the event in over twenty years.

She lived at the beach in southwest Florida and I lived in the mountainous central part of Pennsylvania. *Wow, Florida,* I thought. *And at the beach, too.* We did not dwell on the stark differences in our home lands, but instead moved on to discuss things we had in common. Yes, we had both enjoyed the seminar thus far, were a little sad it was the final day, and grateful we could attend.

Suddenly the coat check ladies magically reappeared at the counter. Not wanting to keep those in line behind me waiting, I forced my attention to the matter of checking my heavy coat. Pam had been right; it did not take long for them to take my coat in exchange for a slip of paper with a number on it.

We were still in conversation after Pam's transaction was completed so moved away from the kiosk together. I thanked her again for the nice gesture as we parted ways—

her to the restroom and me into the seminar room. I moved easier, unencumbered by the weight and bulk of my coat, toward hall "B" to enjoy the final session. I double-checked the sign over the massive doorway. Yes, I was in the right place.

I glided through security then past the joyful, smiling hosts bordering the entrance to the auditorium. Once inside, I was enveloped in the room's cavernous space. The elevated expanse and soft echoes of voices filled my awareness. I was floating on a cloud; occupying the wonderful space with all my senses tuned to the experience.

I looked around at the people pouring through the entrance filling the room, wondering how they would all find open chairs. I glanced toward the front of the hall and noticed others—having come in early—were sitting expectantly facing the stage. Some were twisted sideways in their seats, engaged in discussion with their neighbors. The din of joyful conversation was a blanket of love around me, replacing the coat I had left outside the hall.

Out of the corner of my left eye I saw a waving hand. It was my friend Judy, whom I had just seen in line moments before. She was sitting alone way in the back among a group of chairs on risers. The seats were elevated to give those sitting far from the stage some measure of an enhanced vantage point. For a moment, I thought about joining her, but quickly dismissed it. I waved back gesturing I would be moving forward. It was a half hour before the program began so was hopeful there would still be some seats available closer to the stage.

My engineering mind clicked in to help in my quest. Since the entrance was on the right side, most people would have picked those forward seats closest to it. So, I walked to the opposite side of the hall and then moved forward, scanning each row for the perfect spot.

I found it—only a few rows back from the reserved seating at the front. My plan had worked, there were plenty of open seats since the left side of the hall was less crowded. I chose one midway into the row. It was perfect. I had a good view of the stage and also, a large screen television was positioned directly in front of me so I could see the live video feed even if someone blocked my view of the stage.

A moment later I noticed Judy sliding down my row. Apparently, she had watched me secure a pretty good seat and decided to join me. *Awesome*, I thought. Not only a great seat, but I can catch up with an old friend.

We had not talked long when Judy raised her arm and waved again. I turned to see that she was motioning to the nice lady from the coat check line. *What a coincidence*, I thought, *I'd just met Pam and now she was getting ready to sit next to me. And, evidently, she knew Judy also.*

With Judy on my right and now Pam on my left, I knew this was the place I was supposed to sit. What a delight. Pam and I talked briefly about meeting in line.

"How do you know Judy?", I asked.

She shared that they were in a workshop together earlier in the seminar and had become fast friends.

Things then started to feel very different. The same woman I had a casual conversation with in the coat check line suddenly shared a subtle warmth as we spoke. Something had changed. My brain started clicking, telling me I knew her somehow—and there was no stopping it. There was a familiarity about Pam and I was definitely intrigued.

Poor Judy, I don't think I said a single word to her after Pam sat down. We had about twenty minutes before the start of the morning session and we made the most of it.

Judy did divert my attention briefly by pushing a yellow note pad my way.

"Jeff, put down your phone number and email address on this sheet", she firmly said.

I tore myself away long enough to grab the pen out of Judy's hand then quickly scratch my cell number and email onto the small page. Grateful, I handed the pad back and thanked her for taking the time to think about me. It was nice she wanted to keep in touch.

All too soon the event was ready to start. The twenty minutes Pam and I spent talking seemed more like two.

I turned in my chair to face the stage but my body would not go all the way forward. A strange magnetic pull was coming from the chair to my left and I was unable to place my full attention on the announcement saying the program was about to begin.

What's going on here? I said to myself. I worked even harder at paying attention to the speaker, but I was fighting a losing battle.

First on the morning's agenda was a twenty-minute HU song. It's an incredible experience to sing HU with thousands of others in the same hall. I was looking forward to it that morning—it's a fantastic way to set my feet and attention on the highest point to begin the day.

Once again, I struggled to face forward, then closed my eyes and got comfortable in my seat. Inhaling deeply, I attempted to settle down. I placed my attention gently on the inner screen of my mind and expectantly focused there as we began. There was a problem, however. Yes, I began the HU along with everyone else, but after singing for less than a minute I was no longer able to utter a sound.

The magnetic pull I experienced moments earlier with Pam ramped up to an unimaginable torrent. Continuous sheets of white lightning struck my inner screen—choking out all else in my world. I was rendered totally speechless.

Beyond the light a thick, stone, arched door burst open.

My mind stuttered trying to focus again on the HU, but it was no use, the power within was forcing my consciousness open. The Holy Spirit was coming through loud and clear with Light, and then came the Sound. A tornadic wind howled in my ears—drowning out the thousands of singing voices.

Spirit wanted me to pay attention. It had something to show me.

Beyond the white emanating through the archway I saw Pam. Her highlighted figure gazed loving, compassionately, and directly at me through the opening.

With my consciousness cracked wide open, the howling wind sucked me through the portal, into blankness.

On my inner screen an expansion of my sight and hearing took on a new dimension as my whole world opened up. A vastness. Nothing, yet everything.

Pam and I would be together.

I saw it.

I felt it.

Us, as Soul, as my heart overflowed with love.

It was truth without explanation.

I saw our past.

Our future.

A deep understanding that came in electric waves, like frames rotating in a slow-motion movie.

I felt her.

I felt her love.

And I returned that love to her.

All of her. All of me. Every cell.

My bursting heart showered unconditional love.

I knew in that eternal moment that I had walked through the door, never to return as the same person who had entered. It was a one-way trip and there was no going back.

All the while, my mind was fighting to regain control of the situation. It tried relentlessly to get my attention back to singing HU. My mind, doing what it does naturally, wanted to control my state of awareness. "After-all", it whispered, "that's what you're here for, right? To sing the HU song."

The vision, however, would not let go that easily.

Eventually, I could resume singing. I know not how long I spent in the mesmerizing space beyond the open door. It mattered little, the experience was timeless. I had been lifted above the time track and shown an eternal event, one that would echo through the heavenly worlds down to my earthly existence.

In fact, everything in my outer life was about to change. Yes, on the physical too, there was no going back to life as I knew it before the seminar.

Eventually the HU song was over. I sat in shock for a moment trying to deal with what had just happened. I wondered if Pam had a similar experience.

Slowly I opened my eyes. The relatively dull pale light of the room seemed odd. Just moments before, I was immersed in a brilliant light of 1,000 suns shining in unison. Now, the dimly lit seminar hall pulled me back down to earth—back into the physical world, and also into the arena of the mind.

Now, the human mind is a wonderful tool for survival in this world of the senses. It tries to solve life problems in methodical ways, like a machine. I suppose in early times, the mind and its constant companion, the human brain, served man well. After-all, if you see a tiger and know from past experience that a tiger is a threat, the brain can snap into action to protect you from being its next meal.

The mind can also be a problem. It loves, and craves, routine. The safest places, to it, are ones you have already been to. You know your life, you know what to expect, so you feel safer there. The mind protects from unknown threats. Even if current circumstances are not ideal and are no longer serving us, we tend to cling to them because they are familiar and "seem" safe.

After the HU ended, my mind stepped in trying to erase what had just happened. "What are you thinking", it said. "Everything is okay. Don't upset the apple cart, just keep on with things the way they are." My mind fought tooth and nail with the realization Pam and I would be together and that our lives would be joined going forward.

The resulting confusion left me befuddled, riding an emotional roller coaster. The vibration throughout my body pushed tears to the surface.

Hold it in, Jeff. Don't cry, I pleaded with myself. *Just act normal. Try to act normal.*

The morning session continued for another hour, but I have no clue what went on. I was partaking in a private battle with my mind—first, attempting to reconcile what had just happened, and second, trying to fit that into my future.

Eventually the session came to an end as a voice captured my attention with a few closing words. I had heard them a million times. But somehow, this time, they hit me hard—penetrating directly into my fragile heart.

At that point, I could not stop the tears. Love poured into me like the tide rolling in and filling up an estuary. The water sought to level every nook and cranny, leaving no space untouched by that love.

I was going to need it. It would be this love that would protect and sustain me through the tumult to come. My mind finally stepped aside for a moment of knowingness—it would not be able to protect me through the state of change that was ahead. Only the love of God would get me through.

Somehow, I got ahold of myself and I could speak. Pam and Judy both agreed the morning session was wonderful.

"Yes, it was", I agreed. Secretly, I knew the term "wonderful" was a massive understatement.

Pam picked up our conversation, asking what I was doing after the seminar. I think I said something to the effect of getting to the airport to catch a plane home, or something like that. You see, my mind had been taken off track by the staggering vision and was not able to develop a coherent response.

Inwardly, I knew Pam and I were destined to be together, but outwardly I had no clue how it was going to happen. I guess I figured I would just go back to my life as it was and see what happened next.

Shocked and distracted, I uttered quick goodbyes then turned to walk away.

I shuffled through the crowd in a daze. The din of conversation around me was ethereal. My feet, one in front of the other, were robotically taking me forward out of the convention hall. Once again, tears began to flow. *What just happened?* I asked myself again. *How is this ever going to happen? I can't just change everything.*

I was married. Sure, things had gotten rough recently. Just thirty days before the seminar, I decided I was going to leave the marriage—it had sadly run its course. I even planned possible locations to move to—and had pretty much decided on an area perfect for my current job. Also, I remembered my two boys were all grown up and out of the house. College football, and going to see them play, were things in the past. Still, my mind tried to tell me it would be okay. *Why upset all of this? Just go back and see what happens next.*

I traded a slip of paper for my long wool coat at the check station and managed to make it to the door of the convention center. It was a little warmer, but the wind had picked up. I kept my coat open, not even feeling the cold. Maybe I thought the frigid wind would jolt me back to my senses, make me realize the vision I had of a life with Pam did not really happen at all.

Somehow, I made it back to the hotel. My flight was still a few hours away so I had some time. The coffee shop on the ground floor was my next stop. Yes, a hot cup of brew was definitely in order. Perhaps it would clear my head and allow me to resume my normal life again. Still, the unreality of the moment was present. I felt like I was in a dream. Everything around me had a glow and a hushed silence. At the coffee bar, I blithely spit out my order. "Please add some heavy cream for me", I added. While I waited for the hot liquid to be dispensed, I realized that walking with my coat open had worked, in a way. I was definitely more grounded on this plane—I was freezing.

Coffee in hand, I stumbled to an open seat far from the

busy counter. I wrapped my icy fingers around the cup and closed my eyes, lowering my head as the warmth made its way through the paper-thin container into my hands. I raised the cup to my lips and took a long drink. For me there is nothing like the rejuvenating effect of a warm drink on a cold day. I settled in my seat and took another sip.

I began to reflect on what had just happened, and on the entire week as a whole. This had certainly been a whirlwind trip. Minneapolis, Chicago, back to St. Paul, and then to the seminar here in downtown Minneapolis. What now seemed like it must have been a month, had been less than one week.

My mind jolted back to my current position. I sat there, cup of coffee in hand, trying to shake off the cold and the vision I received during the HU song.

The battle ensued. Part of me wondered how the vision was to come true while another part attempted to erase it entirely.

I did not have time to ponder my next move because the familiar tinkle of my cell phone broke the silence. I slid the hand set out of my coat pocket, squinting at the tiny screen. The number displayed on the caller ID was a Florida number! *Could this be Pam calling me?* I thought to myself. Only one way to know for sure; answer it.

"Hello", I croaked into the phone's microphone.

Sure enough, it *was* Pam, although I could not imagine why she was calling. She said she was also going to the airport and wondered—since I had a car and was headed there myself—if she could have a ride. I mumbled something about the fact that I'd thought to offer earlier ... but since her flight was later than mine ... I figured I'd be leaving way too early for her to be interested in riding along with me. Yeah, it was something cool, calm, and collected like that.

I liked to get to airports plenty early. That way I could just relax and avoid stress about making my flights. She also expressed the desire to get to the airport early. That was probably the one thousandth thing we had in common.

"Sure", I said. "I'll pick you up in a few minutes in front of the convention center."

I hung up the phone. Apparently, *this* was the reason I had written my contact information on Judy's yellow pad. If I hadn't, Pam would not have had my number.

So, this is what happens next, I thought, *Pam and I will share a ride to the airport.*

Secretly, I really appreciated the fact that she called me. I was certain she probably debated quite a bit about phoning, since we had already discussed the airport thing during the morning session. Also, I do not think I could have been any happier at the prospect of picking her up and riding to our next destination together. It just seemed "right".

I think I must have set the world record for hotel check-outs. Before I knew it, I was dragging my bag across the parking lot and sloughing it into the hatch of the Chevy Spark. I jumped into the driver's seat and twisted the key, bringing the tiny engine to life. After a few clicks on the screen of my phone, I had a map and driving directions to the main door of the convention center. Pretty easy, just follow the voice assistant and I am there.

Well, you would have thought I had just won the Powerball jackpot. My energy level was through the roof. The experience during the HU had been reignited by the phone call I just received. And now I was on my way to pick Pam up. Just the two of us; in the tiny private space of my rental car.

I am not sure how what happened next could possibly have taken place. A seminar with thousands of attendees had just ended thirty short minutes ago. With all the busses and cars jockeying for a spot right in front of the convention center, I figured it would be a long time until I could pull in. And even then, I would have to crane my neck trying to spot Pam hiding somewhere in the crowd; probably struggling with her bag.

That is not what happened, however. Miraculously,

there was not a single car—nor a single bus—waiting in front. Also, Pam was standing alone at the curb right in front of me. It seemed like I was just picking her up in front of her home. Very leisurely. Piece of cake.

I jammed the car into park and jumped out. I grabbed her bag and nestled it in the back next to mine, then held the passenger door open for her as she got into the small car.

When I closed the door, I paused.

Something hit me.

At that moment, I realized this was to be the beginning of the rest of my life.

I have often compared the direction of inner guidance, or Spirit, to a GPS device. You set a destination into the machine and touch a button. The machine figures out the best and most direct way in which to get there and begins at step one. Example, get out on the road and turn west.

Life is like this, you set your feet upon a course of action, a goal. If you are tuned in, you watch and listen for guidance on which way to go next. Getting the mind and the emotions to go along with the voice of Spirit can be the challenge. We all have preconceived ideas and norms that can drown out our inner voice. The call of logic can be a powerful side tracker. Spirit has infinite patience with us, however.

I sing HU. The sound can lift me above the babel of my mind and emotions, shifting my state of awareness above the mental and emotional planes into the place where my ultimate guide awaits to help me unfold spiritually. I sure was singing HU *that* morning. Not only during the session, but in those moments afterward when my destiny was fighting with my mind and emotions. Singing HU allowed me to hear the directions from God's GPS more clearly.

With shaking hands, I managed to find my little smart phone again. This time, I called upon the map to get me to the MSP airport rental car return. The device, however, would prove mostly ineffective in guiding me to the destination I had wished for. Thank goodness we had allowed plenty of time because with the distraction of Pam in the passenger seat, I think I missed about every turn I was supposed to make. Thankfully, the voice coming out of the tiny speaker was also infinitely patient. Following each wrong turn, the energetic assistant recalculated the perfect course to guide me to our destination.

Life is similar to this aspect of the GPS as well. We all seem to take "wrong" turns but this is the nature of life here in this earthly shell. We make a decision and the Holy Spirit simply, and patiently, recalculates the best course for us to take. If we are aware and listening then we have another opportunity to get things right and move forward in our spiritual unfoldment.

If my GPS would have been a person with a normal personality, there would have been quite of bit of sighing and admonishment going on. It was a miracle I made it to the rental return for the airport. Too bad it was the *wrong* terminal. You see, the MSP airport has two main terminals. It is like two airports fused together and connected by a rail line. For whatever reason—with all the re-routing going on—the little app had given up on the original destination and had decided "Let's just get this guy to the airport before he ends up in the wrong city"!

Between the synergy and voluminous conversation—while trying to move into the correct lanes—the *exit here and merge left* instructions proved too much for me to handle, I guess. I kept apologizing to her for each wrong turn. *She must think I'm just a bumbling fool*, I thought to myself.

Pam just laughed, shrugging it off joyfully. We talked about the phone call and her asking for a ride. Amazingly, she had received a strong inner nudge to call me. Also, she did not feel our time hanging out together was through. Thank **God Judy** had been there and demanded I write down my number.

I do not think I was ever so glad to get to where I was

going before. Happy just to be at the right company's car rental return line, I could not care less that we were at the wrong terminal. They would check me out and that is all I needed.

Free of the car, and the arduous task of trying to drive while following the directions of my electronic navigator, I was now able to focus on the conversation—focus on getting to know Pam better.

Getting to the *right* terminal from the *wrong* one was an adventure in itself. The signs in the airport seemed to conflict with each other. Still making wrong turns, we finally decided to stop and ask someone for assistance. Eventually, we ended up on the rail line on our way to the correct destination. With each wrong turn, we laughed. We decided this trip to the airport gate was one of life's adventures and were thrilled to be along for the ride.

Once inside the Lindbergh terminal, we pulled out our tickets.

"We're both leaving from terminal F", I said.

"I depart from 3F", Pam stated casually.

"Hey, I'm leaving from gate 3F, too", I excitedly replied.

Turns out, our flights were leaving from the exact same gate! Mine first and hers next, right after mine. What were the chances of *that* happening, we laughed? Two airports jammed together with hundreds of gates and we happen to share the same departure spot. All the while, traveling to two very different parts of the world.

We took it as a divine gift from Spirit; a waking dream symbol. A clue on life's road that we were, in-fact, on the right course.

We both instantly knew sharing the same departure gate was a sign of things to come that would help bring us together. As it turns out, this was only the beginning of an extensive parade of signs and symbols that would assist me and Pam both in navigating the events that needed to take place in order for this to happen.

Since there was still plenty of time before my flight departure, we decided to have some lunch. She offered to buy mine out of gratitude for the ride to the airport. Like I did back in the coat check line, I accepted. Once seated at the airport bar and grill, we placed our orders. We ordered the exact same meal. *The-exact-same-meal.* I should not have been surprised by the common thread by then.

I know I must have been hungry since I had not eaten much for breakfast and it was well past noon, but I was not really interested in food. I managed to choke down half of my salad. In between bites of the tasteless meal, Pam and I talked endlessly—delving into deep topics. Already well past pleasantries, the conversation advanced beyond what new friends talk about. The comfort level was high and we could have talked about anything, except my vision during the HU. I had not even come to terms with it myself yet.

It was time to say goodbye when the flight crew announced final boarding.

Leaning against the wall next to our departure gate, I did not know how I was ever going to get on that plane. Our journey together had just begun. We embraced for a long moment. I held her and for the first time, felt her warmth. I also felt a twinge of sadness. I would be stepping onto that plane without a plan to see her again.

It had been a challenge, certainly, for Spirit to make this happen. I had walked away from her at the coat check line only to have a chance meeting with Judy to bring us back together inside the seminar hall. After the morning session and my vision of us together occurred, I had walked away again.

Next was the extended ride to the airport with all the missed turns and ending up at the wrong terminal. With every delay, Pam and I were getting to know each other more and more.

Finally, Spirit had arranged for us to leave from the same departure gate at the airport. This allowed us to maximize our time together before returning to our respective homes.

I shuffled through the ticket line at my gate then headed onto the plane. The stale air inside the cabin, and the closed-in space, made it seem like a prison. I squeezed past the other occupants and dropped into my window seat. I sat in stunned silence, while the plane taxied away. At least when airborne, I would be able to peer out the window at the open space.

Reflexively, I pulled out my phone and swiped down on the lock screen for one last notification check, since they would soon ask me to turn off my device. I had received a two-part text message from Pam. In the first one she said she was grateful to have a new friend. The second one expressed sadness in watching my plane taxi away.

I smiled to myself and settled back into my seat. This, I knew, would certainly be an interesting journey.

Jeff & Pam Terrell

12

LEAVING

Jeff's Question: What Was My Next Step?

*L*ove offers us many gifts. We are best able to recognize and take full advantage of them by living in the moment—being "present", wherever we are. If we are paying attention, there could be a clue to better understand our lives or even give clear directions for a next step.

I was struggling mightily with a question about my future and it was hitting my head like a hammer. The mind is not the most pliable of instruments, it likes to remain in the grooves that have developed over time and does not really like change.

Two weeks before, I had met the most wonderful woman and been shown that she would be coming into my life in a big way.

But first things first, it was time to resolve my current relationship. Sure, just over a month earlier I had made the decision to leave the marriage and was looking for a new place to live. I struggled to figure out my next move. Spirit was clearly leading me to make a change—now sooner than later—but what? How? When? So much uncertainty.

What was my next step?

A routine trip to the supermarket is where the voice of God spoke to me. I did not need to visit a church or trek across the world to study at the feet of a guru, instead the temple of God was right where I was—even in the parking lot of a grocery store.

I stopped my car and quickly shifted it into park. I sat, distracted, with a question repeating in my head. I could not fathom all the changes coming but felt assured everything would work out for the best. Still, my mind wanted to chew upon the question, placing doubt and fear into my world.

What was my next step?

The broken record played over and over.

I opened the car door prepared to get out, allowing a chilly breeze inside. The ambiance of the parking lot was now audible. A spotlight illuminated the scene as I distinctively heard two people talking.

"How soon are you leaving?", one man asked.

In a boom voice that rose above all others—blocking out all other sound—I heard the reply.

"One month".

The voices were amplified.

I looked around but saw no one near enough to hear so loudly. Then I spotted two men over on the next aisle. *Were they speaking into a megaphone or something?* There was no other plausible way I could have clearly heard two voices—a row away—in a parking lot. Frozen in my seat, I let that sink in.

Still perplexed by the clear message of the innocent bystanders, I noticed something else. My car stereo was still playing, and on the radio I heard the lyrics "Only the Beginning". It was one of my favorite songs by the band Chicago, which I had heard hundreds of times. But this time I heard it, the refrain stuck in my head.

I paused for a moment and allowed spirit to connect the dots in my consciousness.

Then I knew.

I knew the answer to my question.

I guess I'll be leaving my current home in a month and it will be—only the beginning—of my journey, I said inwardly.

I knew my next step.

I knew when I was leaving.

Golden-tongued wisdom provided the answer to my question. A gift of love from spirit.

Months later when I returned to read the journal entry about this event, I was stunned. As it turned out, I had heard the golden-tongued wisdom in the parking lot on November 8th. Almost one month later, on December 9th, I filed the divorce papers.

Only the beginning.

And a month after that, I changed almost everything else in my outer life including where I lived and my job. Along with those outer shifts, I saw and felt the relationships with almost everyone I knew change in their very nature.

As I walked into the grocery store, I breathed a sigh of relief. Perhaps because the hammer was no longer beating on my head. Or maybe because the fear had turned into expectation. The lightness within I experienced at the seminar had returned and was lovingly leading the way.

Jeff & Pam Terrell

13

The Mission

Pam's Vision of the Mission

I had journaled thoughts, frustrations, insights, and stories over half my life and knew there was a book in my future. A couple blurred visions showed possible themes, but nothing concrete. It was not until I got home from the spiritual seminar in 2013, that the vision become crystal clear.

Ten days after I returned home to Florida, I was settling into my new apartment just a short walk from the beach. I decided to start my day the best way possible—with a twenty-minute HU song. Sitting cross legged on the sofa, I started the HU CD and sang along with a few thousand recorded voices. The vibrant sound pulsed love into the room, cleansing my cozy space. I lightly floated a question about my future in my consciousness and continued to sing. Deeply relaxed, the physical body drifted into numbness. The blackness of my inner screen slowly melted away revealing visions of my future.

Photos flipped rhythmically before me in a brief, yet timeless, moment.

I saw: God sent Jeff because he is what I need

I saw: our synergy, we will do much together

I saw: a public event where we share experiences with others

I saw: us speaking at a seminar

I saw: my mission clearly. My mission is service.
I saw: us being creative together
I saw: *our* book! It was not just my story.
I saw: *love.* Divine, unconditional love
I saw: my true partner

In that split-second I was shown a book cover—and what story was to be shared. I knew the book I was writing was to have a co-author, it was not just me! My inner message saying I would "speak of God" flashed before me. I marveled at finally comprehending exactly what the special words meant, and the honor of fulfilling such a mission.

I cried—during the HU, after the HU, an endless sea of tears. The joy of living a life that finally made sense released years of struggle. I knew the profoundness of the inner pull I had felt since my early teens when the first divine guidance message dropped in.

I suddenly sensed a vague recognition of waypoints I had selected before arriving in this lifetime. Ones that were scattered along the path where I could have stagnated, been content, or even stopped the search. But luckily, a familiarity and intense inner drive kept me moving toward an inescapable feeling I was longing for. As Soul, I longed for unconditional love, even though my physical senses never knew it existed.

The Wedding

Jeff and I were married at sunrise at our very special beach a little more than a year after we met. The beach was empty that morning, except for a slim gentleman with a fishing pole near the shoreline in a non-fishing area. We have walked the sandy shores during sunrise many times and never saw anyone fishing there. That morning, however, the man was not exactly as he was seen. As we stood, husband and wife, looking out onto the shimmering endless water, we knew our inner guide was looking on with us—disguised as a fisherman.

*Bound together
as husband and wife,
we will continue traveling
On the Path of Love—
Divine Love.*

Jeff & Pam Terrell

Part V: Epilogue

Jeff & Pam Terrell

14

Jeff Shares a Spiritual Exercise

We are all on the path of love, whether we realize it or not. The challenge comes in finding the true love within ourselves that marks this divine trail in our lives. There is so much illusion to see through in order to find our way. The path, and the practice of love, opens up infinite possibilities existing in our life, giving us tools we need to blaze a trail through the wilderness of illusion so we can find ourselves as we truly are—Soul, a divine spark of God.

Sometimes important lessons will be pointed out, yet other times challenges might get the best of us. Know that it simply takes more practice to untangle from such situations to see the clear light of God shining through to welcome us home.

I have had multiple instances through the years when I felt overwhelmed by a dilemma. The worry of what would happen made the problem even worse because my mind got involved and came up with some of the worst-case scenarios imaginable. The mind likes to close off any ray of hope and force you to resign yourself to a lesser outcome. One that would defeat you.

It is in times such as these that Divine Love can come to the rescue. If you can take the situation to the altar of Divine Love and turn it over to Spirit, you are allowing a miracle to occur. It is best not to imagine a specific outcome, but simply turn the entire situation over to Spirit and allow it to work its' divine magic. God's will, not mine.

There is an easy exercise I will share to help with this task.

Practice being love every day—at every moment. If you do not know what Divine Love is, or cannot imagine being joyful enough to experience it, then mock-up an image or memory of a time when you *felt* love—and allow it to fill your consciousness. Feel the warmth of the sun upon your face—the cool breeze through your hair—the salty ocean fill your lungs. Feel the peacefulness. If there was a moment when you felt truly free, like there were limitless possibilities, then put yourself there. Then sing HU outwardly, or inwardly to yourself if you are not alone. The first few HU's may seem awkward or like a chore, but soon you will feel the inner tuning align you with your own divine nature. I like to spend twenty minutes each morning with this exercise.

Go about your day and when an emotional situation surfaces, and it will sometimes come up again and again, simply turn it over. What I have experienced is, Divine Love will work things out in a manner that surprises me. An outcome I did not, nor could not even imagine, comes to pass. This is a wonderful gift, an unimaginable outcome in tune with your personal divine mission, in alignment with spirit.

Afterward: Coffee Talk with Pam

What is the deal with all the coffee talk, you ask? It took a while for me to recognize the connection myself. On that cold morning in Minneapolis I chose a hot cup of coffee, the one warming my hands when I first laid eyes on Jeff. The paper cup I balanced symbolized a huge turning point involving my health, mind, and the way I lived going forward.

Unbeknownst to me, Jeff, a self-proclaimed coffeeholic, was ready for his own turning point at the exact same time.

We stood in line, side by side, as the invisible aroma connected us together on this physical plane.

Coffee is a treat we enjoy together—whether at home or our favorite local Starbuck's. That is our favorite place to write about our spiritual adventures to share with our new friends. In fact, half of this book was written and edited at coffee shops in several states.

Is it time to wake up and smell the coffee? Could your journey be calling you? We have demonstrated several examples of how guidance appears for us, hoping you can apply those same principles to find your way—and your answers.

As we sip hot or cold brew, we are filled with warmth and love while sharing this beautifully laid path—one that is illuminated with Divine Love.

ACKNOWLEDEMENTS

Together we would like to thank our three sons Alex, Emmitt, and Oliver. We are inspired by each of you and grateful for the important roles you have in our lives. We wish you each a magnificent journey filled with wonder, joy, peace, and unconditional love.

Thank you, Mom Sandy, for always offering to be there—even though I, Pam, am terrible at picking up a telephone.

Thank you Mom Angela for your enthusiastic love and support. "Doc", thanks for sharing your spiritual journey.

Thank you, Janet Thomas, for being a living example of unconditional love and support. Your unselfish attitude is like no other; always on the sidelines cheering people on, no matter what's happening in your own life. Your friendship is magical.

Thank you, Dr. Jason Schwartz, for your review and editing.

And thank *you*! We are grateful for each seeker we have the opportunity to share experiences with and every person we have been blessed to learn from. Our hearts are full of love for each of you along this amazing Path of Love!

ABOUT THE AUTHORS

Jeff and Pam Terrell experienced a profound divine inner message when they first met at a spiritual seminar in 2013. The vision that was revealed seemed implausible at the time—but within two months came to fruition.

Jeff is a Mechanical Engineer, avid cyclist, and spiritual seeker. Pam loves cooking, hiking, and sharing spiritual stories. They have a passion for healthy living and stay abreast of wellness topics.

Together they enjoy looking for spiritual clues in everyday life, writing, and speaking to fellow seekers to help them recognize their own individual messages, symbols, and paths. They live in Florida and enjoy sunsets, beach walks, and dancing.

Jeff & Pam Terrell

www.ingramcontent.com/pod-product-compliance
Lightning Source LLC
Chambersburg PA
CBHW061946070426
42450CB00007BA/1069